Jean Ingelow

Stories Told to a Child

Jean Ingelow

Stories Told to a Child

ISBN/EAN: 9783337004835

Printed in Europe, USA, Canada, Australia, Japan

Cover: Foto ©Thomas Meinert / pixelio.de

More available books at **www.hansebooks.com**

THE SUSPICIOUS JACKDAW.

STORIES

TOLD TO A CHILD

By JEAN INGELOW

BOSTON
ROBERTS BROTHERS
1868

BY THE SAME AUTHOR.

STUDIES FOR STORIES.
A Book for Girls. 18mo, cloth, gilt. Price $1.50.

A SISTER'S BYE-HOURS.
Seven Stories. 16mo, cloth, gilt. Price $1.25.

POEMS.
2 vols. 16mo, cloth, gilt top. Price $3.50.
Blue and Gold edition. Price $3.00.

ROBERTS BROTHERS,

PUBLISHERS,

Boston.

DEDICATED

TO MY DEAREST LITTLE

EDITH,

BY HER LOVING

AUNT.

CONTENTS.

	Page
The Grandmother's Shoe.	9
Two Ways of telling a Story.	37
Little Rie and the Rosebuds.	51
Deborah's Book.	69
The Life of Mr. John Smith.	87
The Lonely Rock.	97
Can and Could.	107
The Suspicious Jackdaw.	115
The Minnows with Silver Tails.	139
I have a Right.	149
The Moorish Gold.	161
The One-Eyed Servant.	185
The Golden Opportunity.	191
The Wild-Duck Shooter.	217

THE GRANDMOTHER'S SHOE.

WHEN I was a child at school (said a friend of mine) my father had an attack of typhus fever; he had quite recovered again, and it was near the time of the holidays, when two servants took the infection; my parents, fearful of conveying it to me, did not write, and my boxes were packed before I knew how I was to be sent home.

My schoolfellows were gone, and in a disconsolate mood I was gazing into the square, when I was told to come into the drawing-room. There, in place of my nurse, who generally came to fetch me, I saw a stout, comely member of the Society of Friends; she was eating cake and wine with imperturbable gravity, and, when she had set down her glass, and smoothed out her gown upon her lap, she held out her hand, and said pleasantly, —

'Does thee remember me, friend?'

I looked at the matronly cloth shawl, the bonnet, with its pure white lining, the smooth gray hair and comfortable face, but could not remember where I had seen them before, till she added, 'What! doesn't thee remember Thomas W———'s housekeeper?'

Then I instantly exclaimed in the affirmative, evidently to the great relief of 'Madame,' who scarcely knew what to make of her grave visitor, and did not know whether she would trust me with her.

She was housekeeper to a rich Quaker gentleman in our neighborhood, with whose children I had once or twice spent the day in haymaking season, and her now remembered face was connected with visions of syllabub, strawberries, and other delicacies which she had served to us among the haycocks.

'Thee remembers; that's well:' she then added, 'thy father knows I am come for thee; friend Thomas offered to take thee home for a while, and he gladly consented.'

Tears came into my eyes at the thought of not seeing my parents, upon which she said, 'There's Lucy, thee knows, and James, and little Martin, to play with. Thy good parents mean to let the young women be nursed in the house, as they gave what help they could when thy father had the fever; so thee sees there is trouble enough without thy trying to add to it.' With a convulsive effort I checked my sobs, and reflected that, though not going home, I was, at least, leaving school, and that was something. The Friend saw my boxes, dressed me, and took formal possession of me and them; then she carried me off in a post-chaise, remarking that she expected I was going to be a good child, and had said so to Lucy, and James, and Martin, when she came to fetch me.

Could I disappoint Lucy, and James, and Martin? No, certainly not; if they were impressed with the notion that my behavior would do me credit, they should find it so.

This was a very good, kind Friend; she let me pay the turnpikes myself, through the window; she bought buns for me; and, by dint of questioning her, I discovered that Lucy, and James, and Martin had got a pony, a donkey, some guinea-pigs, gardens of their own, a swing, and O, joy of joys, a little mill that would go round and grind corn.

By the time I had been welcomed in this hospitable house, and had helped to grind corn in the marvellous mill, I was only a little sorrowful; and by the time I had laid my head on the pillow, in a tiny bedroom next to Lucy's, I felt very much reconciled to my fate, though I knew that I should probably sleep there several weeks.

I was ten years old, and Lucy, a prim little creature, was about the same age; her brothers were quite little children; the other members of the family consisted of a grandmother — a very stern, severe person, whom I greatly dreaded — the master of the house (her son), concerning whom I only knew that he was extremely kind and benign to us, and that he was a widower; and, lastly, his eldest daughter, the child of his first marriage, a sweet girl, little more than twenty years old, but wearing already the clear, high cap in which a really pretty face looks prettier than in almost anything else, and having about her the peculiar self-possession and composure of manner so often seen among those of her society.

Lucy and I were a source of great interest to one another; we liked to be together, because of the different manner in which we had been taught to express ourselves. We examined each other's clothes, and when we had a convenient opportunity tried them on. When this amusement failed we unpacked my toys, but none of them pleased Lucy till we came to two good-sized dolls, dressed in the ordinary costume of British babies; these we no sooner found than we thought how delightful it would be to dress them up in complete suits of Friends' clothes. It was a very rainy day; so we went to the eldest daughter—'sister,' as the children called her—and asked her for some pieces of silk, and scraps of cloth. She was very bountiful, and gave us some pieces of ribbon besides. We took our treasures, our little red work-boxes, and the dolls, to a room in the roof—a large, partially empty place, where we were sometimes allowed to play—and there, with infinite care and pains, we made each of them a dove-colored silk gown of the most approved shape, a muslin handkerchief, a three-cornered brown shawl, and a proper silk bonnet. When the clothes were finished, we wetted the hair of the dolls to take out the curl, and then dressed them, and took them down into the hall, where we walked about with them by way of giving them an airing. I never saw Lucy's father laugh heartily but once, and it was on that occasion; the sight of the 'Puppet Friends,' as he called them, quite overcame his habitual gravity; unluckily, we presently met Lucy's grandmother, who was far from regarding them with the same good-humored indulgence, and it was a painful fact to us, at the time, that after we were gone to bed, the 'Puppet Friends' mysteriously disappeared.

Where they went to we never could discover, though we shrewdly suspected that the grandmother knew; but the mystery was never cleared up till after I returned to school, when I found them among my clothes, neatly wrapped in silver paper, but divested of their Quaker clothing.

I passed a happy week, and on Sunday was sent to spend the day at the parsonage. About six in the evening I was brought back, and Lucy, and James, and Martin ran out to meet and welcome me in rather a more noisy and riotous fashion than suited the day; we were pursuing one another round the flower-beds when 'sister' made her appearance at the window, and calling to us, reproved us gently for our mirth, saying to me, 'What would thy good mother think, if she could see thee just now?' She then set the youngest child upon a chair, smoothed his soft hair, and said to him, with a quietness of manner which soon communicated itself to him, 'Thee must not forget whose day this is; sit there. I am going to read to thee and James about little Samuel in the temple.'

She then took up two Bibles, and gave Lucy and me a parable to learn by heart, sending us up to the room in the roof, and saying, that when she thought we had had time to learn it she should come and hear us say it.

Up stairs Lucy and I accordingly went to the room in the roof, the aspect of which is still as vividly impressed on my mind as if I had seen it only yesterday. It was a very long room, and had a sloping roof, but there was no carpet on it, and no furniture, excepting two square stools, on which Lucy and I sat. The casement windows, both open, for it was hot, afforded a fine view over the country; from these we could look down into the tops of some elm trees, and see a mother rook feeding her young in the nest.

At the opposite end to this the floor was raised one step, and across this raised part was drawn a heavy red curtain, so as to enclose it and the oriel window within it, and make them almost into a distinct apartment. We were forbidden to enter this desirable little place, because it was considered to belong specially to the grandmother; but I had peeped into it several times, when the curtain was partly undrawn, and seen a little table with a great Bible upon it, an arm-chair, and a stand of flowering balsams and geraniums.

The circumstance that this little retreat belonged to the grandmother made me, in common with her descendants, regard it with something like awe. I cannot quite understand why we so much feared this old lady; she did not punish us; she did not scold us; I am inclined to think that we were daunted by the general air of disapproval with which she regarded us, more than by any fear that she would manifest it in deeds or words.

However good we might be, still we were ONLY children. We actually felt ashamed of ourselves in her presence to think that we were children! We knew we could not help it, it was an inevitable dispensation, but she did not appear to think so; she sometimes had the appearance of thinking that we could help it if we liked, and were children on purpose!

Children are inferior beings; we felt that, and were

humble. We are beings whose nature it is to crumple tucks, make finger-marks on doors, run instead of walking, to be troublesome and want looking after, to play with toys and break them. In fact, if one only considers this subject, children take more nursing, more looking after, than one supposes; one generation is almost entirely occupied in teaching, bringing up, and providing for the next. Children, in some way or other, make the talk, the care, and the work for their elders; and if such a thing as an elder is now and then found who does not like children, what an unlucky thing it is for both parties?

But to leave these speculations. The sun was shining in at the oriel window when Lucy and I entered the long white-washed room on that memorable Sunday evening. The red curtain was half drawn, and it cast a delightful glow over the wall; we could not see the window, but we knew it was open, because a slight waft of air from it now and then swayed the curtain up and down, and floated the fallen leaves of geraniums across the bare floor.

We sat down at a distance from the curtain, each on one of the low stools. Lucy smoothed out her clean frock over her knees, set her little feet together, folded her arms, and counted her verses; there were ten. She produced from her pocket a Tonquin bean, two slate pencils, and seven ivory buttons; these she laid out on the floor beside her, taking up one and returning it to her pocket for each verse that she knew; this, she said, made it much easier to learn them. Not to be behindhand with her, and having some faith in the plan, I gathered up ten geranium leaves for the same purpose, and we both set to work to learn our verses with great diligence and gravity.

For some time we persevered, but it was a very warm evening, which, in addition to our being children, was, perhaps, the reason why, at last, we began to yawn, and to fidget, and then to compare notes as to how much we had each learned.

Lucy's bean and pencils had gone back into her pocket, but her buttons lay still in a shining row. We bent our eyes again upon our books — one button went into Lucy's pocket. Then we took a rest, and watched how far the little wafts of wind were floating in the leaves; a great red leaf was following two delicate white ones; it seemed to pursue them; it was a lion running after two lambs; now they lay still, and the lion was watching his prey; now they were borne a little farther; now the lion was just upon them, in another instant they would be overtaken. Lucy could not bear to see the catastrophe that her own imagination had suggested, and darted across the room to rescue the two white lambs; then I related to her Mrs. Cameron's story of 'The Two Lambs,' and by the time it was finished we had so far forgotten ourselves that we went on talking and chattering as if the Bibles had not been lying open on our knees, and as if it had not been Sunday evening, and as if we had neither of us been taught any better.

Oblivious also that there was such a person as a grandmother in the world, we had been talking about my blue sash, and Lucy wished she had one like it. We talked about Lucy's lessons, and I wished I was a Friend, that I might escape from learning music. We talked about the two dolls, about Lucy's sister, and my mamma, which was the most indulgent, and which was the prettiest. We talked about what we intended to do when we were grown up. Last of all, as I well remember, we talked about the grandmother herself, her best gown, her walking-stick, how upright she sat, what a trouble she thought us, whether there was any chance of her going to Ireland to visit her other son; how she often said to father, 'Thomas, thy children ought to be kept stricter — stricter, Thomas;' how, once when she said it, father had smiled, and then grandmother had said, 'Thomas, I fear thou art a light man.' 'And we saw father smile,' said Lucy, shrewdly; but the words were scarcely uttered when the smile died out from her own face, and a sudden blush mounted to her forehead. 'What is it, Lucy? what's the matter?' I exclaimed. Lucy sat as still as if she scarcely dared to breathe; she seized my arm to check me, and pointed towards the curtain. Alas! shame and fear soon flushed my face as red as her own, for the terrible conviction struck us that the grandmother was behind it; the curtain had been blown a little backwarder than before by the summer wind, and peering beyond it in the sunshine was the toe of a shoe that could belong only to the grandmother!

Never shall I forget the sensations of the next few minutes, nor the sudden silence that succeeded to our childish and profitless talk. We did not expect to sit there long; every moment we looked for a summons from her to come into her presence and receive the lecture which we knew we so richly deserved; but when that imperturbable shoe had kept its position a little longer, we almost wished she would break the silence, that this fearful suspense might be ended. But no, she neither stirred nor spoke; the most perfect quiet reigned; there was only a slight rustle now and then, which might be the turning over of a page, and which we had heard before, supposing it to be only the curtain.

We did not know what to do, we were so miserable. We gazed intently through the red folds of the drapery, and could see, by a dark shadow, that the chair was occupied. O that we had but been wise enough to notice this before! We withdrew our eyes, and, with one tearful look of condolence at one another, dropped them again upon our verses, and began to learn them with extreme diligence and humility. But still the inexorable grandmother never spoke. O, how startling would be her voice when it came!

Not a word either of us said for a long time. At length Lucy observed, in a humble, saddened voice, 'I know my parable; Sophia, dost thou?'

I had learned mine perfectly for some time, but neither of us rose. We had an idea that the first attempt on our part at leaving the room would be met by the dreaded summons; we were already enduring punishment of a very severe nature; our cheeks were dyed with shame, and our hearts beating with apprehension. At length we heard a distant step sedately and steadily mounting the stairs; now it was coming along the uncarpeted passage, then a hand was on the door, and 'sister' entered, asking us, with her usual

sweet gravity, whether we knew the parable she had
set us.

She paused for a moment, evidently surprised by
our troubled, shamefaced expression; but she asked
no question, and, to our utter confusion, advanced
straight to the curtain, as if to pull it back. 'Sister,
sister!' exclaimed Lucy, springing forward, but not
in time to prevent what she was doing; she flung
aside the curtain, and O, inexpressible relief and
astonishment, no grandmother was there!

We had both risen; and now the full sunshine
streamed up over the ceiling and rested on sister's
quiet forehead; it did not fall low enough to reach us;
we were left in shadow, but the shadow had passed
away from our hearts. She said to Lucy, 'Why didst
thou check me, child?'

Lucy replied with a sigh of relief, ' I thought grandmother was there.'

We entered the little sanctum, saw how the grandmother's garden shawl and bonnet were thrown over
the chair, remarked her garden over-shoes, which had
frightened us, the scissors with which she had dressed
her plants, and the gloves lying beside her Bible; then
we looked at one another with feelings of gratitude, and
followed sister to the grandmother's chair, where she
sat down while we stood before her and repeated our
parable. As she sat there, her tall figure slightly bending forward, the open Bible lying upon her knee, her
serene eyes fixed on ours, and the sweet sunshine
touching her soft hair and tranquil forehead, she presented a picture which is indelibly impressed upon my
memory, together with a sense that I had of the con-

trast between her peace and my own consciousness of misdoing. She returned the Bibles when we had finished, saying to me with serious sweetness, 'I am pleased with thee; thou hast learned thy verses well, and said them reverently.'

She again looked at us as if puzzled by our faces, and then she rose and would have left the room, when we stopped her, for her praise was not to be received when we knew we did not deserve it. We asked her to sit down again, and then half laughing, half crying, related the whole of our adventure; we concealed nothing; we told over all our conversation, how we had been chattering and playing, what we had said about the grandmother, our terror and shame when we thought we were in her presence, and our indescribable relief when we found she was not there.

Much as we respected sister, we so wanted her to sympathize, that, though we knew she would disapprove of our behavior, and perhaps reprove us, we by no means softened our tale in the relation, but described how every rustle of the curtain had disturbed our guilty consciences; how we had sat upright on our seats, not daring to look about us, so conscious were we of the grandmother's presence, even though we knew she could not see us.

Sister looked from one to the other with an expression of regret, but not the least tendency to a smile. 'I thought grandmother would never forgive us, and she would tell father,' said Lucy, 'how we had played and laughed, and talked about her, and all on First-day evening. I was so ashamed I wouldn't have

THE GRANDMOTHER'S SHOE.

had her know for anything. I thought I should never be happy again.'

'And, after all,' I added, 'there was no harm done.'

'No harm!' said sister, quietly, 'what dost thou mean?'

'Why, you know,' said I, carelessly, 'the grandmother was not there.'

'Thou heedless child,' she answered, with that look of pity and regret, 'art thou really so much afraid of my grandmother, and dost thou wholly forget the ear that *did* listen to thy talking, and the eye that *was* upon thee all the time?'

We both looked about us, at the curtain, at the places where we had been sitting, and in sister's face, with a sudden sense of the presence and nearness of God, that I believe we had never felt before. When she added, 'What wouldst thou have done if, when I drew back the curtain, thou hadst seen the Redeemer standing there? Shouldst thou have said then there is no harm done?' We neither of us answered a word, so completely were we surprised into awe by the aptness of this word in season.

'Years have passed since then,' said my friend, 'but I believe the effects of that gentle rebuke have not altogether passed away with them; it made a greater impression upon us than even the grandmother's anger could have done, however great that might have been.'

When 'sister' had left us, we went to one of the open casements, and I well remember the sensation of repose with which we congratulated one another on the grandmother's not having been present; and though the consciousness of a far higher presence was strong in our hearts, we experienced also somewhat of that feeling which made King David say, 'Let us fall now into the hand of the Lord, and let us not fall into the hand of man.'

In our childish fashion we began to speculate as to how we should behave if we always believed and remembered that the Great God was observing us; and then, as I suppose, most children have done at some time or other, we suddenly formed a resolution, that from that day forward we would behave quite differently; that we would reform all our faults, never be idle over our lessons; nor play at improper tunes, nor conceal any mischief that we might have done; nor tease the little ones, nor hide ourselves in the shrubberies when we knew the nurse was looking for us to call us in to bed.

In short, we passed in review all our childish faults as far as we knew them, and made a set of rules for future good behavior.

We had a fashion at the school where I was for writing sets of rules; one would have thought the rule under which we lived was stringent and inflexible enough; but no, we copied Madame's favorite phrase, 'I shall make a rule, *Mes Demoiselles*,' and we made more rules than even our rulers.

We often spent part of one half holiday in writing rules for the spending of the next — elaborate rules, as to how long we would play with our dolls, how long we would spend over our home letters, how long in reading our story-books, how long in feeding our birds;

in short, we had scarcely one half hour which we could call our own that we did not hamper with rules containing as many additions and subtractions as a long division sum. I had imparted this fashion to Lucy, and we had already made, and altered, and broken several sets of these rules, but, on that delightful Sunday evening, while the sun was sinking into the distant sea, and reddening the sky, the water, the walls, our white frocks, and the fluttering leaves of our Bibles, we made one set more. The particulars of them I have forgotten, but the intention formed, in all childish simplicity, was to help us to keep the presence of God always in our recollection.

There was a little picture in one of my books which represented Hagar in the parched wilderness sitting apart from the fainting Ishmael; underneath it were the words, 'Thou, God, seest me.' This, we said, we would hang on the wall opposite to our two stools, where every afternoon we sat learning our lessons for the next day, or doing our playwork, as we called it.

How little, for all the sympathy of love, a child is known to his elders! How little during the ensuing week our childish troubles, our wavering endeavors to do right, our surprise at our own failures, were suspected in that orderly household! The days, however, went and came, and our rules it appeared must have had some real influence over us, for I well remember that the nurse and housekeeper commended us to 'sister' as 'excellent good children, as toward, friend, as thee would wish to see.' The restrictions which we had laid upon ourselves were not light ones for children to observe, and, though they only bound us to do our duty, it was not wonderful that we sometimes broke through them, and sometimes lightly forgot them, considering that the red curtain did not always hang in our sight, and considering that childhood and youth are vanity.

Another Sunday evening came; we learned our lessons in the upper room, and were so quiet and diligent that the presence of no grandmother in the world could have frightened us.

The next morning we were awakened early by the rooks in the trees, close by our windows, and we rose and went out for a ramble before breakfast.

Within the grounds, which were laid out partly in grass and flowers, and partly in shrubbery, there was a walled fruit-garden; and this we were only permitted to enter on the express understanding that we were on no pretence to gather, or to pick up, or to touch any of the fruit; 'not so much' (so 'sister' phrased it) 'as a fallen gooseberry.'

Fruit was always given to us once during the day, but the father of the family was extremely particular about his trees, and suffered no fruit to be gathered but by his own hand.

I was told of this regulation at once by the children, and when Lucy said to her sister, 'Did thee know that Sophia had leave to gather fruit at home?' and I exclaimed, that I did not wish to do it here, and was very happy; she answered with her usual sweet composure, 'Thee need not blush so much, I know thou art in general a reasonable child.'

'I don't wish for anything,' I explained, 'that Lucy does not have.'

'That's well,' she replied; 'we desire to see thee happy and satisfied; but thou knowest that my father considers thee under his authority while thou art here, and will not alter his rule for thy sake; but as thou hast been used to gather fruit for thyself, I advise thee not to go into the fruit-garden, if thou art tempted to transgress. There are other walks where thou canst bowl thy hoop.'

'I wonder you should suppose such a thing,' I interrupted, quite vexed at her plain speaking, and the implied supposition that I could be tempted to such a greedy and disobedient act.

She smiled at my speech, but there was nothing sarcastic in the smile; and she answered, 'I do not suppose thee to be any better than thy first mother; yet she was tempted with an apple.'

'And apples are not half so good as plums,' observed one of the little brothers, sagely nodding his head.

'No one asked for thy opinion,' said my champion Lucy, in a low voice; 'does thee wish Sophia to be kept out of the garden?'

Sister cut the conference short, by giving us each a piece of seed-cake, and sending us out with general directions to be good, and not get into mischief; and there was such ample space to play in, and we had so many means of amusing ourselves, that we should have been more culpable than most children, if we had disobeyed them.

The garden, with all its walks, the orchard, where we sometimes sauntered early in the morning, and saw the greengages which had fallen in the night lying among the dewy grass; the rough trunks of the plum trees all gray with lichen, and blue above with partly ripe fruit, are vividly impressed upon my recollection; as well as the frames on which, in the middle of the day, we sometimes laid our hands to feel how hot the glass was; peeping through at the long cucumbers and plump melons, as they lay basking in the moist heat; or following the gardener when he walked round with his tiles, and laid them carefully under those which he wished to ripen first.

I also remember, as if it had happened but yesterday, how we used to run to meet Lucy's placid father, as he came leisurely down the grass walk, to have his daily colloquy with the gardener; how he gathered and stored the ripe pears from the espaliers, and lifted up the leaves from the wall fruit to see how it was coming on; how he would lament that birds should be such arrant thieves, and turn a deaf ear to the old gardener, when he muttered that there was but one way to cure them of it.

Then I remember the cool fruit-house, into which we sometimes helped him to carry summer apples; and what the gardener called the 'kippen peers;' but above all I remember a certain fine young apricot-tree, a moor-park, in its first year of bearing, and how every day we went to count and admire upon it six beautiful apricots, and no more.

Few things in a garden are more beautiful than ripening apricots; the downy surface, the rich golden color, speckled, as in this sort, with clear red spots, and surrounded by pointed leaves of most glossy green, and broad sunshine that bathed them, the careful training,—

all combined to make us take a peculiar interest in this young tree, which had been the only survivor among several of the same sort that had been planted along with it.

When we had walked all round with Lucy's father, he used to take up a flat straw-basket, lay some leaves of curly brocoli in it, and go with us to the orchard, where he would gather some ripe greengages, purple plums, jargonel-pears, with, perhaps, a few late whiteheart cherries, and some little red apples, red to the very core. In the south wall of the garden there was a door, leading into a place they called the wilderness; it was an uncommonly well-ordered wilderness, like everything about the premises. Through this door father used to proceed to a bench under the trees, where he caused us to sit down in a row, while he divided the fruit equally among us.

There was no underwood in this delightful retreat; the trees composing it were elms, thickly boughed plants to shelter us from the sun, but not to prevent the elastic mossy grass from flourishing underneath, nor to prevent the growth of numerous groups of large white lilies.

All the lilies in the garden had done flowering, but these, more pure and more luxuriant, through shade and shelter, were then in their full perfection, and filled the air with their delightful fragrance.

The children called them sister's lilies, because when she was a child she had planted them.

We generally brought pieces of bread with us, to eat with our fruit, and the wilderness being our favorite retreat, we played there at all times in the day.

The lilies were taller than the younger children, who would stand on tip-toe to push their little fingers into the higher flowers, and bring them down covered with yellow pollen.

Unchanged, themselves, in their white purity, they were yet susceptible of apparent change from difference in the light cast upon them. When the full glare of high noon was upon the tops of the elms, then was cast, through their leaves, upon the lilies, a faint tinge of most delicate green; but at sunset, we, who lived so much among them, sometimes saw a pure glow of crimson reflected through the white petals, when the setting sun sent his level beams between the trunks of the trees. But I have said enough of these fragrant lilies, they are dead now, and the hand that planted them.

As I before mentioned, after that successful Sunday, Lucy and I walked out in the garden early in the morning, and congratulated one another on our good behavior, which we intended always to last, and firmly believed it always would; but we were growing careless and confident, and though the thought of the red curtain never failed to bring salutary feelings with it, there were times when we did not think of it at all, and in one of those times temptation came.

It was fine weather, and we expected some cousins of Lucy's to spend the day with us, and, as we walked, we planned how we would pass the time. Lucy confided to me that they would most likely be very noisy, and perhaps rude; but this, like two little self-righteous Pharisees, as we were on that particular day, we decided to prevent if possible; certainly not to participate in, as Lucy said she often had done hitherto.

I believe we had not the least idea that our strength might fail us, and we made our arrangements with as much composure as if we ourselves were quite above the ordinary temptations of humanity.

The cousins arrived soon after breakfast, and the very first sight of them dissipated some of our ideas; they were older, had more assurance of manner than ourselves; but children understand each other so well that I perceived, even during the first half-hour, that they were amusing themselves at my expense, and taking notice of every word I uttered, as was evident by the glances which passed between them, though to outward appearance they were remarkably grave. I also observed that Lucy, though so accustomed to see them, and though she talked of them so freely in their absence, was very much awed by them, and very silent now.

When they escaped from the presence of their elders, their manner suddenly changed; they had evidently not been brought up like ourselves, and their gravity and over-submissiveness in the company of their uncle, and their riotous behavior in his absence, had a bad effect upon us all.

At first, Lucy and I were all blushes and deference; but they soon laughed us out of that, and by means of a little well-applied ridicule brought us into such complete thraldom, that, though we neither liked them, nor enjoyed playing with them, we wished nothing so much as to stand well in their eyes, and to be and to do whatever they chose to dictate.

It is astonishing what mischief can be done in a day! Two rough boys, and one prim little girl, so upset our ideas of right and wrong, and frightened us out of propriety, that we were nearly as rude as themselves through false shame at appearing otherwise. We heard the father laughed at in his absence, and ridiculed for his peculiarity about the fruit, and we had nothing to say; we saw sister seeking for us in the shrubbery, and eluded her, and had lost courage against their orders to come out of our hiding-place and show ourselves. Yet these cousins kept us in high spirits, or rather in a state of considerable excitement; we spent the whole day with them in games of play, and went to bed at night thoroughly tired, and not at all inclined to talk together as usual.

At six o'clock the next morning we got up and went out into the garden; the excitement of the past day was still upon us; we were not at all like the children who had walked there previous to this visit.

It was a very sultry morning, the air was still, the dew was dried already from the grass. It wanted an hour yet to breakfast time, and as Lucy and I sauntered leisurely through the wilderness, we discussed her cousins, blaming them very freely in their absence, though we had wanted courage to do it at the proper time.

We passed into the walled garden, and there the heat, for the time of day, was quite remarkable; we got under the shade of the wall, and took off our bonnets to use by way of fans. Apples, pears, plums, lay thickly under the trees; the neighborhood of the frames was fragrant with the scent of the melons, which seemed as if it might have been collecting there all night, for there was not the least waft of air to carry it away. We came to the little apricot-tree, and stopped before it as usual; the six apricots were now quite ripe. Lucy was quite sure her father would gather them that day, and hoped he would give one to us.

We were just about to pass on, when, O sad mischance! a ripe one fell heavily from the highest branch at our feet, and broke nearly in half with the force of the fall. It was not one of the six, we counted them, and all were in their places; a tuft of spleenwort grew out of the wall just where it fell from; behind that and some leaves this apricot must have ripened, and been entirely concealed.

Before we knew what we were about, Lucy had picked it up and divided it. 'Look,' she said, 'father does not know of this, and the wasps would spoil it before he came out; eat thy half, and I will eat mine.' She put it into my hand, and I immediately tasted it and ate it.

I cannot say that even in eating that apricot was nice to the taste; it was imbittered by conscience; and hot as the morning was, it did not refresh me.

A short silence followed; we remained standing before the apricot-tree; then, without looking each other in the face, we moved slowly to the door into the wilderness.

Broken rules and regulations began to rush back into my recollection, with shame, and repentance, and regret, till Lucy, suddenly bursting into tears, and exclaiming, 'O, I am so sorry, Sophia! I am so sorry I gave it thee!' I turned to look at her, and saw in her hand the other half of the apricot. Her face was crimsoned through agitation, the cause of it was evident, when she added, that if I wished it she would now eat the other half, for, as she had tempted me, I should not be alone in the punishment.

I was far from having any such wish; she had hesitated at the right moment. Unhappy as I was, it would have been no relief to know she had as much cause for sorrow as myself. I asked her to give me the other half of the apricot, and we found a little space bare of grass at the foot of a lily, where we made a small hole and buried it, and covered it down.

When we had done this Lucy appeared relieved; but as for me, every moment increased my uneasiness; I wondered, I was astonished to think, that for such a very paltry gratification I should have put my neck under such a yoke; either I must conceal this fault, and be always in fear lest it should be discovered, or I must confess it — confess to greediness, a fault children feel peculiar shame in — and not to my own father, but to a gentleman whose hospitality I was enjoying, who gave me as much of his fruit as he thought good for me every day, and who allowed me to play in his garden, only on the express promise on my part that I never would take any without his leave. All this, and much more, passed through my mind, as we walked slowly in to breakfast. I thought not only of my fault with reference to man, but having such slight experience as yet in the frailty of my nature, I wondered how it was that when it most behooved me to remember it, I should have forgotten our resolution when we found ourselves free from the consequences we deserved at the drawing back of the red curtain, and wondered more than all that I should have forgotten the saying that hung so often in my sight, 'Thou, God, seest me.'

We entered the house and found breakfast ready; the heat was wonderful, and the stillness in the air was complete. A singular glow was diffused over everything, though the sun was not shining, and through the open window came multitudes of minute flies like morsels of black thread.

Sister said there was going to be a storm; we all felt oppressed. Lucy was quiet, but a restless feeling of apprehension hung over me. My mind was busy with the young apricot-tree, and in every face I fancied I saw a reflection of my thought.

It was impossible to keep the flies off the bread; the tea was sprinkled with them, as well as the tablecloth and our clothes. The grandmother presently began to tell how such a swarm had preceded a great storm which took place in her youth, when a house was struck, and a bed driven into the middle of a room, while two children who were sleeping in it remained uninjured.

The wearisome meal at length was over, the poor little children were quite overpowered; the youngest came up to his sister, and leaning his head against her, said, 'I want to sit on thy knee.' As she took him up, James and Lucy brought their stools to her side, and looked in her face apprehensively.

'What art thou afraid of?' she said composedly to Lucy; 'GOD IS IN THE STORM, He can take care of thee.'

The father and grandmother went out of the room

to give some orders, and the next instant several vivid flashes of lightning seemed to dash across our faces. 'There,' she said, when the thunder which followed them ceased, 'dost thou see how quiet Sophia is?— She is not afraid.'

'I am not afraid of the storm,' I replied; and I asked her if I might go up to my own room.

She gave me leave, and I moved up stairs to the little chamber. I remember something of the terrible dimness which seemed to have gathered in an instant; and of the glowing heat that appeared to strike against me as from the door of an oven. But sister's remark that God was in the storm, was paramount to everything else, and before the thought of safety came the necessity to ask forgiveness.

Let no one say my fault was a trifling one; it was the same which had cost my first mother her place in Paradise. I had eaten forbidden fruit; and as I knelt at the foot of the bed and hid my face, I remembered what sister had said on this subject, and how I had despised her advice to keep away from temptation.

Again, there rushed over my heart the sudden comprehension of the nearness of God. In my childish thought I felt His presence so close to me, that I did not need to pray aloud; but as well as I could I entreated forgiveness, though the deafening peals of thunder seemed to drown my words, and confuse my very thoughts and senses. The floor shook under me, and I heard the furniture rattle and reel; but God, I knew, was in the storm, and gradually, as I prayed to Him, His near presence, which had been so terrible to me, became, to my apprehension, a source of rest, and brought a consciousness of protection.

There was nothing else to trust in during that great danger; but it was enough. I was quite alone, and though sometimes a little stunned by the noise, was able to distinguish the strange sounds, the creaking and crashing of boughs of trees, the lowing of the frightened cattle, the distressed cries of the rooks. The very house itself seemed endowed with power to complain, and groaned and trembled to its foundation.

One other incident I remember of that half-hour: something soft had brushed across my hands; I lifted up my face, and saw two trembling, dripping swallows sitting on my pillow!

And now the sound of drenching rain was added to the tumult of the thunder. I remained kneeling, but was no longer afraid. Then came a short pause, and I thought I would get up and look for Lucy's father. I did not doubt that my fault was forgiven, but my head was still a little confused with the noise, and I wished to tell him my fault without considering whether this was a convenient season.

I wandered about, but could find no one; I opened several doors; at length I came to the upper room so often mentioned, advanced to the red curtain and looked in. There I saw him and the grandmother sitting side by side, perfectly composed, but with somewhat awe-struck faces; the son was holding his mother by the hand, and they were quite silent. I came in and stood beside him for a few minutes; the storm was clearing off with magical celerity, and two minutes after the last tremendous clap of thunder, the rain ceased, and the sun shone out over the sodden grass and the ruined garden, all strewed with broken branches, fallen fruit, and dead nestlings flung from the nests, and over which the mother rooks were piteously lamenting. The great fear of God so lately suffered, had taken away for a time all fear of man; and though the grandmother was present, I did not feel afraid when I asked Lucy's father if he would hear something that I wanted to tell him.

Some few things in our childhood make such a deep impression on the mind that they are never forgotten. I still remember how I told my story to Lucy's father, and almost the very words in which I told him.

I remember his benign face, which, to my great surprise, never once became in the least displeased all through the broken narrative. I remember the grandmother's manner, which, stranger still, never reproached me as it did at other times. I remember the touch of her aged hand, as once or twice she passed it softly over my hair; and, more than all, I remember the quiet kindness of Lucy's father, and how gently he said, when I had finished, and he had reflected for a few moments on my tale, 'Well, well, let him that is without sin among us first cast a stone at thee.'

From that day forward the grandmother was particularly kind to me.

TWO WAYS OF TELLING A STORY.

WHO is this? A careless little midshipman, idling about in a great city, with his pockets full of money.

He is waiting for the coach: it comes up presently, and he gets on the top of it, and begins to look about him.

They soon leave the chimney-pots behind them; his eyes wander with delight over the harvest fields, he smells the honeysuckle in the hedge-row, and he wishes he was down among the hazel bushes, that he might strip them of the milky nuts; then he sees a great wain piled up with barley, and he wishes he was seated on the top of it; then they go through a little wood, and he likes to see the checkered shadows of the trees lying across the white road; and then a squirrel runs up a bough, and he cannot forbear to whoop and halloo, though he cannot chase it to its nest.

The other passengers are delighted with his simplicity and childlike glee; and they encourage him to talk to them about the sea and ships, especially Her

Majesty's ship *The Asp*, wherein he has the honor to sail. In the jargon of the sea, he describes her many perfections, and enlarges on her peculiar advantages; he then confides to them how a certain middy, having been ordered to the mast-head as a punishment, had seen, while sitting on the top-mast cross-trees, something uncommonly like the sea-serpent — but, finding this hint received with incredulous smiles, he begins to tell them how he hopes that, some day, he shall be promoted to have charge of the poop. The passengers hope he will have that honor; they have no doubt he deserves it. His cheeks flush with pleasure to hear them say so, and he little thinks that they have no notion in what ' that honor ' may happen to consist.

The coach stops: the little midshipman, with his hands in his pockets, sits rattling his money, and singing. There is a poor woman standing by the door of the village inn; she looks careworn, and well she may, for, in the spring, her husband went up to London to seek for work. He got work, and she was expecting soon to join him there, when, alas! a fellow-workman wrote her word how he had met with an accident, how he was very ill, and wanted his wife to come and nurse him. But she has two young children, and is destitute; she must walk up all the way, and she is sick at heart when she thinks that perhaps he may die among strangers before she can reach him.

She does not think of begging, but seeing the boy's eyes attracted to her, she makes him a courtesy, and he withdraws his hand and throws her down a sovereign. She looks at it with incredulous joy, and then she looks at him.

TELLING A STORY.

'It's all right,' he says, and the coach starts again, while, full of gratitude, she hires a cart to take her across the country to the railway, that the next night she may sit by the bedside of her sick husband.

The midshipman knows nothing about that; and he never will know.

The passengers go on talking — the little midshipman has told them who he is, and where he is going; but there is one man who has never joined in the conversation; he is dark-looking and restless; he sits apart; he has seen the glitter of the falling coin, and now he watches the boy more narrowly than before.

He is a strong man, resolute and determined; the boy with the pockets full of money will be no match for him. He has told the other passengers that his father's house is the parsonage at Y——, the coach goes within five miles of it, and he means to get down at the nearest point, and walk, or rather run over to his home, through the great wood.

The man decides to get down too, and go through the wood; he will rob the little midshipman; perhaps, if he cries out or struggles, he will do worse. The boy, he thinks, will have no chance against him; it is quite impossible that he can escape; the way is lonely, and the sun will be down.

No. There seems indeed little chance of escape; the half-fledged bird just fluttering down from its nest has no more chance against the keen-eyed hawk, than the little light-hearted sailor boy will have against him.

And now they reach the village where the boy is to alight. He wishes the other passengers 'good evening,' and runs lightly down between the scattered houses. The man has got down also, and is following.

The path lies through the village churchyard; there is evening service, and the door is wide open, for it is warm. The little midshipman steals up the porch, looks in, and listens. The clergyman has just risen from his knees in the pulpit, and is giving out his text. Thirteen months have passed since the boy was within a house of prayer; and a feeling of pleasure and awe induces him to stand still and listen.

'Are not two sparrows (he hears) sold for a farthing? and one of them shall not fall on the ground without your Father. But the very hairs of your head are all numbered. Fear ye not, therefore, ye are of more value than many sparrows.'

He hears the opening sentences of the sermon; and then he remembers his home, and comes softly out of the porch, full of a calm and serious pleasure. The clergyman has reminded him of his father, and his careless heart is now filled with the echoes of his voice and of his prayers. He thinks on what the clergyman said, of the care of our heavenly Father for us; he remembers how, when he left home, his father prayed that he might be preserved through every danger; he does not remember any particular danger that he has been exposed to, excepting in the great storm; but he is grateful that he has come home in safety, and he hopes whenever he shall be in danger, which he supposes he shall be some day, he hopes, that then the providence of God will watch over him and protect him. And so he presses onward to the entrance of the wood.

The man is there before him. He has pushed himself into the thicket, and cut a heavy stake; he suffers the boy to go on before, and then he comes out, falls into the path, and follows him.

It is too light at present for his deed of darkness, and too near the entrance of the wood, but he knows that shortly the path will branch off into two, and the right one for the boy to take will be dark and lonely.

But what prompts the little midshipman, when not fifty yards from the branching of the path, to break into a sudden run? It is not fear, he never dreams of danger. Some sudden impulse, or some wild wish for home, makes him dash off suddenly after his saunter, with a whoop and a bound. On he goes, as if running a race; the path bends, and the man loses sight of him. 'But I shall have him yet,' he thinks; 'he cannot keep this pace up long.'

The boy has nearly reached the place where the path divides, when he puts up a young white owl that can scarcely fly, and it goes whirring along, close to the ground, before him. He gains upon it; another moment, and it will be his. Now he gets the start again; they come to the branching of the paths, and the bird goes down the wrong one. The temptation to follow is too strong to be resisted; he knows that somewhere, deep in the wood, there is a cross track by which he can get into the path he has left; it is only to run a little faster and he shall be at home nearly as soon.

On he rushes; the path takes a bend, and he is just out of sight when his pursuer comes where the paths divide. The boy has turned to the right; the man takes the left, and the faster they both run the farther they are asunder.

The white owl still leads him on; the path gets darker and narrower; at last he finds that he has missed it altogether, and his feet are on the soft ground. He flounders about among the trees and stumps, vexed with himself, and panting after his race. At last he hits upon another track, and pushes on as fast as he can. The ground begins sensibly to descend — he has lost his way — but he keeps bearing to the left; and, though it is now dark, he thinks that he must reach the main path sooner or later.

He does not know this part of the wood, but he runs on. O, little midshipman! why did you chase that owl? If you had kept in the path with the dark man behind you, there was a chance that you might have outrun him; or, if he had overtaken you, some passing wayfarer might have heard your cries, and come to save you. Now you are running on straight to your death, for the forest water is deep and black at the bottom of this hill. O, that the moon might come out and show it to you!

The moon is under a thick canopy of heavy black clouds; and there is not a star to glitter on the water and make it visible. The fern is soft under his feet as he runs and slips down the sloping hill. At last he strikes his foot against a stone, stumbles, and falls. Two minutes more and he will roll into the black water.

'Heyday!' cries the boy, 'what's this? O, how it tears my hands! O, this thorn-bush! O, my arms! I can't get free!' He struggles and pants.

'All this comes of leaving the path,' he says; 'I shouldn't have cared for rolling down if it hadn't been for this bush. The fern was soft enough. I'll never stray in a wood at night again. There, free at last! And my jacket nearly torn off my back!'

With a good deal of patience, and a great many scratches, he gets free of the thorn which had arrested his progress, when his feet were within a yard of the water, manages to scramble up the bank, and makes the best of his way through the wood.

And now, as the clouds move slowly onward, the moon shows her face on the black surface of the water; and the little white owl comes and hoots, and flutters over it like a wandering snowdrift. But the boy is deep in the wood again, and knows nothing of the danger from which he has escaped.

All this time the dark passenger follows the main track, and believes that his prey is before him. At last he hears a crashing of dead boughs, and presently the little midshipman's voice not fifty yards before him. Yes, it is too true; the boy is in the cross track. He will pass the cottage in the wood directly, and after that his pursuer will come upon him.

The boy bounds into the path; but, as he passes the cottage, he is so thirsty, and so hot, that he thinks he must ask the inhabitants if they can sell him a glass of ale.

He enters without ceremony. 'Ale?' says the woodman, who is sitting at his supper. 'No, we have no ale; but perhaps my wife can give thee a drink of milk. Come in.' So he comes in, and shuts the door; and, while he sits waiting for the milk, footsteps pass. They are the footsteps of his pursuer, who goes on with the stake in his hand, and is angry and impatient that he has not yet come up with him.

The woman goes to her little dairy for the milk, and the boy thinks she is a long time. He drinks it, thanks her, and takes his leave.

Fast and fast the man runs on, and, as fast as he can, the boy runs after him. It is very dark, but there is a yellow streak in the sky, where the moon is ploughing up a furrowed mass of gray cloud, and one or two stars are blinking through the branches of the trees.

Fast the boy follows, and fast the man runs on, with his weapon in his hand. Suddenly he hears the joyish whoop — not before, but behind him. He stops and listens breathlessly. Yes, it is so. He pushes himself into the thicket, and raises his stake to strike when the boy shall pass.

On he comes, running lightly, with his hands in his pockets. A sound strikes at the same instant on the ears of both; and the boy turns back from the very jaws of death to listen. It is the sound of wheels, and it draws rapidly nearer. A man comes up, driving a little gig.

'Halloa?' he says, in a loud, cheerful voice. 'What! benighted, youngster?'

'O, is it you, Mr. Davis?' says the boy; 'no, I am not benighted; or, at any rate, I know my way out of the wood.'

The man draws farther back among the shrubs. 'Why, bless the boy,' he hears the farmer say, 'to think of our meeting in this way. The parson told me he was in hopes of seeing thee some day this week. I'll give thee a lift. This is a lone place to be in this time o' night.'

'Lone!' says the boy, laughing. 'I don't mind that; and if you know the way, it's as safe as the quarter-deck.'

So he gets into the farmer's gig, and is once more out of reach of the pursuer. But the man knows that the farmer's house is a quarter of a mile nearer than the parsonage, and in that quarter of a mile there is still a chance of committing the robbery. He determines still to make the attempt, and cuts across the wood with such rapid strides that he reaches the farmer's gate just as the gig drives up to it.

'Well, thank you, farmer,' says the midshipman, as he prepares to get down.

'I wish you good night, gentlemen,' says the man, when he passes.

'Good night, friend,' the farmer replies. 'I say, my boy, it's a dark night enough; but I have a mind to drive you on to the parsonage, and hear the rest of this long tale of yours about the sea-serpent.'

The little wheels go on again. They pass the man; and he stands still in the road to listen till the sound dies away. Then he flings his stake into the hedge, and goes back again. His evil purposes have all been frustrated — the thoughtless boy has baffled him at every turn.

And now the little midshipman is at home — the joyful meeting has taken place; and when they have all admired his growth, and decided whom he is like, and measured his height on the window-frame, and seen him eat his supper, they begin to question him about his adventures, more for the pleasure of hearing him talk than any curiosity.

'Adventures!' says the boy, seated between his father and mother on a sofa. 'Why, ma, I *did* write you an account of the voyage, and there's nothing else to tell. Nothing happened to-day — at least nothing particular.'

'You came by the coach we told you of?' asks his father.

'O yes, papa; and when we had got about twenty miles, there came up a beggar, while we changed horses, and I threw down (as I thought) a shilling, but, as it fell, I saw it was a sovereign. She was very honest, and showed me what it was, but I didn't take it back, for you know, mamma, it's a long time since I gave anything to anybody.'

'Very true, my boy,' his mother answers; 'but you should not be careless with your money; and few beggars are worthy objects of charity.'

'I suppose you got down at the cross-roads?' says his elder brother.

'Yes, and went through the wood. I should have been here sooner if I hadn't lost my way there.'

'Lost your way!' says his mother, alarmed. 'My dear boy, you should not have left the path at dusk.'

'O, ma,' says the little midshipman, with a smile, 'you're always thinking we're in danger. If you could see me sometimes sitting at the jib-boom end, or across the main-top-mast cross-trees, you *would* be frightened. But what danger can there be in a wood?'

'Well, my boy,' she answers, 'I don't wish to be

over-anxious, and to make my children uncomfortable by my fears. What did you stray from the path for?'

'Only to chase a little owl, mamma; but I didn't catch her after all. I got a roll down a bank, and caught my jacket against a thorn-bush, which was rather unlucky. Ah! three large holes I see in my sleeve. And so I scrambled up again, and got into the path, and asked at the cottage for some beer. What a time the woman kept me, to be sure! I thought it would never come. But very soon after Mr. Davis drove up in his gig, and he brought me on to the gate.'

'And so this account of your adventures being brought to a close,' his father says, 'we discover that there were no adventures to tell!'

'No, papa, nothing happened; nothing particular, I mean.'

Nothing particular! If they could have known, they would have thought lightly in comparison of the dangers of 'the jib-boom end, and the main-top-mast cross-trees.' But they did not know, any more than we do, of the dangers that hourly beset us. Some few dangers we are aware of, and we do what we can to provide against them; but, for the greater portion, 'our eyes are held that we cannot see.' We walk securely under His guidance, without whom 'not a sparrow falleth to the ground!' and when we have had escapes that the angels have admired at, we come home and say, perhaps, that 'nothing has happened; at least nothing particular.'

It is not well that our minds should be much exercised about these hidden dangers, since they are so many and so great that no human art or foresight can prevent them. But it is very well that we should reflect constantly on that loving Providence which watches every footstep of a track always balancing between time and eternity; and that such reflections should make us both happy and afraid — afraid of trusting our souls and bodies too much to any earthly guide, or earthly security — happy from the knowledge that there is One with whom we may trust them wholly, and with whom the very hairs of our head are all numbered. Without such trust, how can we rest or be at peace? but with it we may say with the Psalmist, 'I will both lay me down in peace, and sleep, for thou, Lord, only makest me dwell in safety!'

LITTLE RIE AND THE ROSEBUDS.

LITTLE RIE AND THE ROSEBUDS.

THE last house before you come to the open heath is a gray, cheerless looking place in winter, though in summer it looks pleasant and gay, for it is nearly covered with china roses.

There are a good many trees in the front garden, and some thick laurestinus shrubs. On one side of the porch is the kitchen casement; on the other side the parlor windows. All through the summer, rose leaves drift in whenever these are open, and, even as late as November, rosebuds tap against the glass whenever the blustering gale comes round from the heath, as if appealing to the inmates to take them in and shelter them from the wind and the rain.

The inmates are a mistress and a maid. The former is a widow; but her late husband saved money in his trade, and has left her a comfortable annuity. The latter is not very fair, nor very wise, but, as her mistress says, her honesty makes up for want of wit, and she has a kind heart, though it be a foolish one.

One dreary November afternoon, when the sky was piled up with cold, white clouds, and the gusty wind shook every pool in the gravel walk into ripples, the mistress came into the kitchen and sat at a table stoning raisins for a cake, while the maid kneaded dough for the said cake in a pan on the window-seat.

Suddenly a shadow darkened the window, and mistress and maid raising their eyes, saw a dark, determined-looking woman standing outside offering matches for sale; she held a tiny child about five years of age by the hand. The little creature peered with childish interest into the kitchen, and she also pushed forward her bundle of matches; but they were perfectly wet, and so was the dimpled hand that held them, for rain was streaming from every portion of her tattered garments.

'No; go away; we don't want any matches,' said the mistress; but the woman still stood before the window with a forbidding, not to say menacing, aspect.

'The woman's boots and clothes are very good,' said Sally, the maid; 'but it's pitiful to see the poor child's bare feet and rags; she looks hungry, too.'

'Well, Sally, you may give her something to eat, then,' said the mistress.

Sally rose with alacrity, and rubbing the flour from her arms, ran hastily to a little pantry, from which she presently returned with a piece of cold pudding. She opened the casement, and held it out to the child, who took it with evident delight and began to eat it at once. Then the dripping pair moved away, and the mistress and maid thought no more of them, but went on with their occupation, while the short day began to close in the sooner, for the driving clouds and pouring rain, and the windows in the little stone house began to glow with the cheerful light of the fires.

In the pauses of the wind and rain, Sally once thought she heard a light footfall, but she did not see any one in the garden, though if any one did come in then and wander round the laurestinus bushes, and sit down in the little porch, that person must have seen all that went on that rainy night in the cheerful little parlor and kitchen; must have seen the white-washed walls of the kitchen glowing with a more and more ruddy reflection from the flames; must have seen the little door open in the face of the cuckoo clock, and the cuckoo start briskly out and sing, and dart in again; and must have seen Sally bustling about, cutting bread and butter, setting out tea-things, and putting on her clean apron; then the person by simply turning, could have seen the mistress, in her afternoon gown and cap, sitting in her pretty parlor, the walls all covered with roses, and the carpet gay with bright flowers.

It grew quite dark. Sally sat making a round of toast at the fire, and just as she turned the toast upon the fork, a little child stole as silently as a shadow from the porch, and pressed her cheek against the glass, and wondered whether there was any more of that nice cold pudding in the cupboard, and looked at the lazy cat as she came and rubbed herself against Sally's gown. But presently the wind came round again, and dashed the rosebuds so hard against the casement, that she was frightened. It seemed as if they rapped on purpose to let people know she was there; and she crept back to the porch, and once more cowered down in its most sheltered corner.

She was very wet; but she did not mind that so

much as might have been expected; she did not mind being out in the dark either, for she was well accustomed to it; but she was very tired, they had walked so far that day; and every minute she looked out into the garden and listened, and wondered why her mammy did not come, for she was alone. After they had left that house in the afternoon, they had walked far out on to the great heath, and had sat down, and then her mammy had said to her, 'Now, child, you may go back, do you hear?' and she had risen and said, 'Yes, mammy, where am I to go back to?' 'It don't much signify,' her mammy had answered; 'you may go back to that little house where they gave us the pudding, and I shall be sure to come soon; I'm a-coming directly.' 'And shall you be sure to find me, mammy?' she had asked; and then her mammy was angry and said, 'Set off directly when I bid you; I shall find you fast enough when I want you.'

So she had set off as fast as she could; but it was a long way, and a long while before she reached the porch, and then she was so tired she thought she should have cried if there had not been a little bench to sit down on.

She called this woman her mammy, but she had a real mother a long way off, of whom this one had hired her, because when they went out begging, her little appealing face made people charitable. What wonder, since the real mother could so give her up, that the pretended one should desert her if she no longer needed her!

But she did not know her desolate condition. She only thought what a long, long time her mammy was in coming, and she crept out of the porch again to see the mistress sitting at work, and stooping now and then to pat a dog that lay basking on the rug at her feet. What a soft rug it was! The beggar child wished she was a pet dog, that she might lie there in the light and warmth; but once more the wind swung a branch or rosebud against the glass, and she withdrew to her comfortless shelter, longing for the time when her mammy was to fetch her.

And then two more dreary hours passed over her head; sometimes she cried a little, and sometimes she dozed, and woke up chilled and trembling; sometimes she took courage, and wandered about among the laurestinus bushes, so fearful was she lest her mammy should miss her; then she went back again and cried, and was so tired she did not know what she should do if she had to wait much longer. At last her little head sunk quietly down upon her knees, and the wind, and the rain, and the darkness were forgotten.

She was sound asleep; but after a long time she dreamed that some one shook her and spoke to her, but she could not open her eyes, and then that little dog began to bark at her, and she was so frightened that she cried bitterly in her sleep. Some one (not her mammy) was lifting her up and carrying her away, and giving her something so hot and so nice to drink, that she was amazed, and could open her eyes and sit up; there was the cuckoo clock, and the little dog; he really was barking at her; but the warm fire was shining on her, and Sally the maid was pulling off her wet clothes, and telling her not to be frightened, and she should have some supper.

Poor little outcast! They dried her trembling limbs and wrapped her in a blanket; but she was so faint and sleepy that she could hardly hold up her head, even while they gave her some supper, but presently fell asleep on Sally's knee over the comfortable fire.

'Well, Sally,' said the mistress, 'I can only say that this is the strangest thing I ever heard talk on.'

'And so it is, ma'am. Please what am I to do now with the little dear?' said Sally, simpering.

'I suppose we must keep her for the night; make up a little bed on three chairs; and I must go up stairs and look out some clothes for her out of the bundle I made up to give away at Christmas.'

So the mistress went up stairs; and then Sally made the little bed, and prepared a warm bath to refresh the aching limbs of the poor little wanderer; and then she combed her pretty hair, and carried her, already asleep, to the little bed on three chairs.

The next morning, when the mistress came down into the kitchen, she saw her baby-guest sitting on a low wooden stool, nursing the cat; her dark hair was neatly brushed, and her face was as clean as Sally's care could make it; her eyes watched with inquisitive interest the various preparations for a comfortable breakfast. Her features expressed a kind of innocent shrewdness; but she was evidently in great awe both of mistress and maid, though, when unobserved, she was never tired of admiring her new checked pinafore, and smoothing out her spotted print frock with her hands.

'Shall I give her some bread and milk, ma'am?' asked Sally.

'Certainly,' said the mistress; 'and after breakfast I shall consider what is to be done with her.'

So the little thing had a good breakfast: and all the morning the mistress sat considering; but at dinner-time it appeared that she had not considered to much purpose, for when Sally came into the parlor to lay the cloth, and asked, 'Am I to give the little dear some dinner, ma'am?' she answered again, 'Certainly, Sally, and I must consider what is to be done; I've not been able to make up my mind. How has she behaved?'

'Been as good as gold,' answered Sally, with a somewhat silly smile; 'she saw me dusting about, and I gave her a duster, and she dusted too, and then stood on the stool and see me making the pie, and never touched a thing. O, she's a toward little thing.'

After dinner it began to rain, and then the wind got up, and the rosebuds rattled and knocked again at the casement. A little before tea-time the mistress felt so lonely that she came into the kitchen for company, and there she saw Sally sitting before the fire, making toast, and the child on a chair beside her, with a small piece of bread on a fork.

'She's toasting herself a bit of bread for her tea,' said Sally, 'leastways, if you mean to give her her tea, ma'am.'

'Certainly,' said the mistress once more. 'Dear me, how cheerful it looks! — doesn't it, Sally? a child seems always to make a place cheerful. Yes, I shall give her her tea, if she is good.'

If to be quiet is to be good, never was a better child; and certainly never was a happier one.

'Have you considered anything yet, ma'am?' asked Sally.

'Why, no, I can't, Sally, just yet; it's so wet, she must sleep here to-night,' replied the mistress. 'I'll think of it to-morrow.'

But to-morrow the mistress still said, 'I'll think of it to-morrow;' and so it came to pass that at the end of a month the child was still there. She had grown plump and rosy, though still extremely shy and quiet, which was in her favor; for mistress and maid finding so little trouble, and such a constant source of amusement and occupation, had gradually dropped all consideration as to what they were to do with her, and thought of nothing less than letting her go away at all.

She called herself little Rie, and said she come from a big place; but that was all that questioning could draw from her, excepting the repeated declaration that she did not want to go back to her mammy.

How happy she was in the pretty kitchen, with Sally, nursing the cat, listening to the tapping rosebuds, sitting on the little stool to eat her simple fare, going to the shop with Sally, and creeping softly into the parlor to peep at the dog, or carry a message or a plate of biscuits to the mistress! She was very happy, indeed, at first, but soon there began to mingle a great deal of fear with her reverence for the mistress. She had been brought up with no habits of order, with no schooling, and now she was to be taught and trained; and every day, when she was sent into the parlor, with a nicely washed face and smooth hair, to say her lesson, and hem a duster, she became more and more shy.

'The poor child's been used to such a roving life,' said Sally, 'that she don't take as kindly as might be to her books. She doesn't learn as easy as other children.'

'And that's the very reason why I'm so particular,' replied the mistress. 'I wonder, Sally, to hear you talk as if you wished her to be excused.'

'I don't know as I do wish that,' said Sally humbly, for she had a great idea of her mistress's good sense; 'but, ma'am, she's such a little one, and you see we often wants excusing ourselves.'

The mistress was a severe person; and though she heartily loved little Rie, and did not mind what trouble she took with her, she could not bear that the child should see any fondness in her manner, lest, as she said, 'she should take advantage.' What she had told her once she expected her to remember; and, above all, she could not bear deception; for she was very upright herself, and expected others to be so too.

But poor little Rie had been used to hard usage, and it was some time before she could be taught that she must speak the truth and confess her faults, whatever might be the consequences. Deceit, once taught to a young child by fear, is not easily eradicated, and Sally thought nothing but kindness could do it; but then Sally had such a foolish way with her, and was all for kindness and making excuses for people, not sufficiently considering what was just, and not being willing to condemn anybody without such a deal of consideration, that the mistress felt she could not take her opinion at all.

'Please, ma'am, she will speak out if she's not afraid,' Sally would say when little Rie had cried herself to sleep, after being punished for some childish deceit.

'Not afraid!' the mistress would repeat. 'How you talk, Sally! I punish her to make her afraid of doing anything else but speak out.'

'But, ma'am, consider her bringing up,' said Sally, ' and don't look for too much at first.'

'Too much!' repeated the mistress; 'don't I give her everything, and haven't I a right to look for obedience and truth in return?'

'Surely,' said Sally, 'and I hope you'll have them, ma'am.'

'I hope so,' replied the mistress; but the very next day little Rie got into trouble again, for she was told to hold out her pinafore while the mistress counted apples into it for a pudding; the pinafore was not half full when the mistress was called away, and then little Rie, left alone, looking at all the bright, rosy apples, lying in rows on the low shelf, found the temptation too great for her, and bit one of them, which she hastily returned to its place. When the mistress came back and found the little culprit, with cheeks suffused with crimson, and head hanging down, she easily discovered what had happened; and then, in spite of her promises that she would be good, she was summarily punished, and put to bed.

'She is but a child,' said Sally.

'She's a naughty child,' said the mistress, 'and it is just she should be punished.'

'Yes, ma'am,' Sally ventured to say, 'only somehow if you're angry when you do it, won't she think you don't love her?'

'Dear me, Sally, how foolish you are! I don't want her to think I love her when she's naughty, but only when she's good.'

'O, don't you, ma'am?' replied Sally, doubtfully. 'Well, ma'am, no doubt but you know best.'

'I must be just,' continued the mistress; 'she shall be indulged when she's good, but I shall never overlook it when she's naughty.'

The mistress was as good as her word; and as little Rie was often naughty in her childish way, it followed that she was often punished; till once seeing her dear Sally crying, after the mistress had been more than usually angry, she climbed up her knee, and made many protestations that she would never be naughty any more and make Sally cry.

Poor little Rie, she had her troubles; but she loved Sally dearly; and perhaps, child as she was, she had sometimes, when the rain was pouring down, and the wind howling outside, a dim perception that she had been saved from a dreary, toilsome, and evil life, and it was strangely better to sit with Sally in the cheerful kitchen, and hear the rosebuds tapping, than to wander down and down those ever lengthening roads, cold, and hungry, and neglected.

But discipline, though it may be harsh, does not fail to produce a certain good result. Little Rie understood very soon that she was never to be punished unless she was naughty; that was, at least, something learned, as it had been by no means the experience of her infantine life. It was a great thing to know that she was never to be punished excepting when she had done wrong, and this, once learned, she did wrong much seldomer, and, as they hoped, had also learned to speak the truth.

And now she had been very good for a long time; and, by consequence, she was very happy, and the time passed rapidly, till all the snow had melted away and the garden was full of crocuses and snow-drops; it seemed only a few days and they were over; and she could watch the rosebuds coming out; and then it seemed a very little time longer before Sally was constantly telling her to pick the roseleaves up and throw them out, when they drifted in at the window.

At last, one day, one sorrowful day, the mistress came into the kitchen to make a raisin pudding, while she sent Sally and little Rie to the shop, and during their absence she twisted up some few raisins in a paper and laid them on the dresser, intending to give them to the child when she came in. But Sally came in very late; and when she laid a rabbit, and a plate of butter, and papers of sugar, rice, and tea on the table, and then proceeded to count out eggs and produce apples and other good things, the mistress forgot the raisins, and pushed back her flour, and all her apparatus, to make room for the groceries. Sally was not a good accountant, and she had scarcely made out the price of each article and produced the change, when some friends came to see the mistress, and she washed her hands and went into the parlor.

When they were gone, she remembered her intended present and came back into the kitchen; she moved every parcel and every dish, searched the dresser, and looked on the floor, but the paper of raisins was not to be found — it was gone.

'Come here, little Rie,' she said gravely; 'did you see a paper of raisins on the table when you came home?'

'Yes, ma'am,' said the child, whose two small hands were tightly clasped behind her.

'And do you know what has become of them?'

'No, I don't, I sure I don't,' replied the child, and her delicate neck and face became suffused with crimson.

'O, my dear!' exclaimed Sally, 'if she'll speak the truth, I know missis won't be so angry with her. O, she will speak the truth, I know.'

'I did, I did,' cried the child, with an outbreak of passionate tears.

Sally upon this searched the floor and tables, and nothing could be more clear than that the raisins were not there. Alas! they could not doubt that she had eaten them, for she had been left alone in the kitchen for a few minutes, and Sally herself admitted that they could not have gone without hands.

'Now, if you will speak the truth,' said the mistress, gravely, 'and confess that you took those raisins' —

'I didn't,' repeated the child, now too much in a passion to care what she said; 'I don't want the nasty raisins, and I won't have them.'

'O, this will never do,' said the mistress; 'Sally, I really must correct her!'

'Will she tell it all?' said Sally, once more stooping over the child, for she had flung herself on the floor, and was sobbing and screaming. But no, little Rie would only struggle and fight her away, till at another bidding she went with a sorrowful heart to fetch the rod, and when she came back she found the child in such a passion, that she ventured no remonstrance, though she still hurriedly looked about with the vague hope that she might have spoken the truth after all.

Poor little Rie! she was very naughty. Sally was the more grieved, because lately she had always spoken the truth; but now, when an hour after her punishment, the mistress came in again, and offered to forgive her on condition of her speaking the truth, she sullenly walked into the corner, and sobbed, and would not say a word.

'Then, Sally, you must go these errands by yourself,' said the mistress; 'I meant to have let her go with you, but now she must stay here by herself.' Little Rie looked up as she went away, and saw that she was very stern and angry. O, how little either of them thought that they should never look one another in the face again!

Sally went away. It was a lovely afternoon, and the kitchen door leading into the back garden was open. Little Rie at first was very disconsolate, but soon the light spirits of childhood began to assert themselves, and she began to play, though very quietly, and with an occasional sob, till at last, O, woful mischance, she knocked down a cheese plate! It fell clattering upon the floor, and broke into fifty pieces;

one moment she stood aghast! then her terrified fancy feigned a step upon the stairs; she darted through the open door and rushed down the garden. Where she should go to escape the anger of the mistress, she scarcely knew; but she came to the garden wicket, it led into a lane; she opened it, shut it behind her, and with it shut the door upon home and hope; shut the door upon all that had kept her from beggary and wretchedness, from a vagrant life, from contact with everything that is evil and vicious, and from ignorance of everything that is good.

She ran away, and no one knew what became of her. There was a man who said, some time afterwards, that he had met her that night about sundown, wandering over the moor, but that he had asked her no questions, for he thought some of her friends must be near at hand. In the course of time many rumors got about respecting her, but nothing was ever known. Little Rie 'was not;' she had vanished from her place like a dream.

O, weary nights, when Sally was alone by the fire, and thought of her pretty companion, and cried, and then started up and opened the door, to find for the fiftieth time that it was only the tapping rosebud that she had heard against the casement! O, weary nights, when the mistress lamented over her, and forgave all her childish faults, and wondered to find how much she had loved her; and could not rest in the wind for thinking of her shelterless head, and could not rest in the rain when thinking of the night when first she took her in, and could not rest in her bed for dreaming of a desolate child wandering up and down, with no one to take her by the hand, or lead her towards heaven!

And yet the mistress did not reproach herself. She had done well to take the child; few would have done as much; and she had done well to punish her; it was just and right that she should suffer for her faults.

But weeks after, when poor Sally's simple heart was getting used to miss the child, the mistress came into the kitchen and took down a little covered jar full of caraway seeds, from a shelf over the dresser; she looked in, and a mist seemed to rise and shut out the sunshine without and within, for there lay the paper of raisins; in an instant she knew it again, and knew that in her hurry and confusion, she herself must have thrown it in. Yes, that little jar had been standing beside her. Then into it she must have pushed or dropped the raisins, and afterwards, with her own hand, she must have set the jar upon the shelf above, to be out of her way.

Miserable, aching pain! How hard it was to have it so often in her heart, and by slow degrees to grow into the knowledge, that even a just punishment may become unjust, unless it is administered in the spirit of love! But hers had not been a just punishment. Alas! she had not possessed herself of any certain knowledge of the fault; she, herself, had outraged that sense of truth and justice which she had been at so much pains to implant; and now there was no means of making restitution.

But let us not judge her; for in this world of uncertain knowledge and concealed motives, how few of us there are not equally at fault! It is not the effect of one particular act of injustice that should impress us with so much regret, as the habit of too great suddenness or harshness in judging. How difficult it is for us to estimate the many ways in which we may be mistaken! When shall we learn to keep the knowledge always present with us, that often kindness is our best uprightness, and our truest justice is mercy?

DEBORAH'S BOOK.

WHEN I was a little child, I thought what a good thing it would be if I could set out on a pilgrimage. I had been reading the *Pilgrim's Progress*, and had specially pondered over the account of the wicket gate. The wonderful book which contains the description, and the picture of it, I had read up in a garret in the house of an old lady, to whom I was paying a visit; an old lady who never came down after breakfast till twelve o'clock, who dined at one, drank tea at five, and after that dozed and dreamed in her easy chair. She lived by the sea-side, and was of kin to my mother. I had been sent alone to her. She did not like children, as she told my parents, therefore she could not ask any of my numerous brothers or sisters to visit her at the same time; but I was a quiet little thing, 'shod with velvet,' and contented to sit still and dream over my book; besides, when I worked I could thread my own needle, and the last child that she had invited to stay with her was always teasing her to ring the bell for Deborah to come in and thread her needle. This had made a deep impression on the old lady, and she would often say, 'If I have rung the bell once for Deborah to come in and thread that child's needle, I have rung it fifty times, my dear.' 'Indeed!' my mother would reply; and add, with pretty maternal pride, 'my little girls are all particularly clever with their needle.'

'So they are, my dear,' our aged relation would answer; and she once added, 'As for this little thing, she mended my gloves the other day like a woman, and then came up to me so prettily, "Are these stitches small enough, do you think, Mrs. Wells? there's rather a long one here, but I can pull it out if you like." "Yes, my dear," said I, "that will do." I couldn't see one of 'em without my spectacles! You may send her to me, and welcome, Fanny, if you like. I dare say the sea air will do her good—a poor little aguish thing.' So I was sent, or rather brought over by my father, together with my knitting and my netting, my little work-box, my story-books, and my *Peep of Day*. I felt what a fine thing it was to go out on a visit, and what a matter of rejoicing it was that my cheeks were not round and rosy, like the cheeks of my brothers and sisters; besides, mamma had put a new blue veil on my bonnet, to shade me from the sun, and had given me a parasol—a thing that I had never possessed before, for I was only six years old. Therefore, as I said, a natural elation resulting from conscious ill-health, and some new property, took entire possession of my little heart; and as I sat in the gig by papa's side, I drew myself up as much as I could, and hoped the passers-by, seeing me with my veil and my parasol, would think I was a grown-up lady.

Mamma had given me five things to remember, and had counted them over to me on the fingers of my hand, after she had put my new gloves on.

I was never to forget to say my prayers; I was to write to her twice a week; I was always to change my shoes when I came in from a walk; I was to keep my room very tidy; and (greatest charge of all, as I thought at the time) I was honestly to tell the housemaid, when I was sent up to bed, that mamma did not wish me to put out my own candle. I was very anxious to persuade mamma that I could put it out myself, therefore she was the more urgent in impressing upon me that she would not allow it; and, in taking leave of her, and during the drive to the sea, I thought very much (when I was not thinking of my veil and my parasol) about that candle.

We reached the house. Mrs. Wells did not come out to meet us, but received us rather cordially, though she reminded my father that he had promised to be in time for dinner, and that he was full ten minutes late; he made some trifling excuse, we sat down to this early meal, and very shortly after my father took his leave. Then, as I well remember, my relative rang the bell, and sent for Deborah. Deborah, a rough, red-cheeked young woman, came in, and her mistress addressed her with, 'Now, Deborah, I hope you haven't forgotten my orders about the garret.'

'No, ma'am,' said Deborah, 'and I've scrubbed it and dusted it, and laid out the half-crown you gave me for toys; and if miss makes all the noise she can there, you'll never hear her.'

'That's right, Deborah,' replied my relative languidly. 'Go up with Miss Rosamond, and show her the room; there, go away, my dear, till tea-time.'

So I went up stairs demurely, not the less so because Deborah kept looking at me; and when we got into the garret I found it perfectly empty, literally empty of furniture, excepting that there was one ottoman footstool on the floor which was heaped with paper parcels.

'Well, now,' said Deborah, addressing herself, 'didn't I say, over and over again, that I would contrive a table for this child — what a head I have!' and so saying, she flounced out of the room, bringing back, in a few minutes, the smooth lid of a very large deal box, and two light bedroom chairs. Setting them some distance apart, she laid the flat lid on their seats, and it made a capital table, just the right height for me to sit before on the ottoman. She quickly picked up the parcels, and laying them on my table, exclaimed, 'There, missy, now see if that is not a good half-crown's worth. Mistress said you were to play up here, and when I told her there was nothing to play with, she said I might go to the shop *down town*, and lay out half-a-crown. See here!'

I opened the parcels, and found in one, to my great joy, a dozen Dutch dolls, with lanky legs, and high plaited hair, fastened with the conventional golden comb that Dutch dolls always wear; in another I found a toy-box of pewter tea-things, and a similar box of lambs upon a movable stretcher; and in two more was a quantity of doll's furniture. I was exceedingly content, the more so when Deborah, going out again, presently appeared with a bandbox full of odds and ends, with which, she said, I might dress my dolls; and two books, with pictures in them. These last, she said, I might look at as often as I liked, but I must not tear them; they were hers. So saying, she left me, and if ever I was happy in my life I was happy then. All by myself, plenty of new toys, a table on purpose for me, and a little window, which, when I stood upon my ottoman and looked out, showed me the long waste of salmon-colored sand, and the bathing-machines left high and dry, and the green sea tumbling at a distance; and the happy little shrimpers with their nets, whose absolute duty it was to do what all children long to do as a pleasure — take off their shoes and stockings and splash about in the warm salt water. What delight to have all these things, and quiet to observe them in, and leisure to enjoy them! The nursery at home had plenty of toys in it, but there were two babies there, who must not be awakened by any games of play while they slept, and when they were awake it always resounded with such laughing and jumping, such pushing and running, such crying, quarrelling, and making it up again (unhappily for this divided world a more easy thing in chidhood than afterwards), that there was no time for enjoying play, and no quiet for reading even the prettiest story. 'Master John, be quiet; your shouting goes through my head; O, deary me, Miss Mary, do sit down and keep quiet; Miss Alice, if you can't leave off that crying, I really must call your mamma,' were the constant complaints heard in our nursery; but childhood, on the whole, is a happy time, though a cross nurse does now and then overshadow it with gloom.

Well, there I was. In due time I was called down to tea, and asked whether I liked my playroom. I said I did, and that I was very happy. My relation answered, as if to be contented and happy was a merit — 'Good child.' After that she gave me some shrimps, and when tea was over sent me out for a walk on the beach. The servant who walked with me was as silent as her mistress. I came home, went to bed, and got up again the next day, still feeling very happy; but the quietude of everything around me was working its due and natural effect in making me quieter still. To meet it, and to harmonize with it, I did not talk aloud to my Dutch dolls, nor scold them in imitation of our nurse's accents; but I whispered to them, and moved about my playroom noiselessly. 'Are you happy, my dear?' asked my relation again, when I came down to dinner; and I answered again, 'Yes, ma'am.' And so several days passed, and the servants, as well as the mistress, praised me, and called me the best and the quietest child that ever came into a house — no trouble at all, and as neat as a nun! But I was beginning to be strangely in want of change. I wished my sister Bella, or even my noisy brother Tom, could see my twelve dolls, all dressed in the grandest gowns possible, and could help me to dry the sea-weeds that I brought in from the sea-beach. On the fourth day I bethought myself of the two books, and I well remember taking one of them to the little open window, laying it down on the sill, and opening it. What a curious picture! A man with a heavy burden on his back, standing before a high gate, and over the gate a scroll. 'Knock,' was written upon the scroll, 'and it shall be opened unto you.' The man seemed to be considering whether he would knock, and a number of angel faces were looking out from among the clouds to see whether he would.

I looked at that picture a long time, then began one by one to examine the numerous woodcuts which adorned the book. There were lions and hobgoblins, and giants, and angels, and martyrs, and there was the river flowing before the golden gates; nothing that could awe the imagination and take hold on the spirit of a child was wanting.

Specially I remember dwelling, with childish reverence, on the picture of the river, and the pilgrim entering into its depths; and pondering over the strange and to me unintelligible meaning of the beautiful words, —

'Now there was a great calm at that time in the river; therefore Mr. Standfast, when he was about half-way in, he stood awhile, and talked to his companions that had waited upon him thither; and he said —

' " This river hath been a terror to many; yea, the thoughts of it also have often frightened me: now methinks I stand easy: my foot is fixed upon that upon which the feet of the priests that bare the ark of the covenant stood, while Israel went over this Jordan.

' " The waters indeed are to the palate bitter, and to the stomach cold; yet the thoughts of what I am going to, and the conduct that awaits me on the other

side, doth lie as glowing coal at my heart. . . . .
I have formerly lived by hearsay and by faith, but now
I go where I shall live by sight, and shall be with Him
in whose company I delight myself.

'"I have loved to hear my Lord spoken of, and
wherever I have seen the print of his shoe in the
earth, there have I coveted to set my foot too."'

Extraordinary words! their pathos and their sweetness reached into my heart even at that early day, though their meaning was shrouded in the veil that gathers round the path of childhood. I hung over the picture, and hoped the man with the solemn face would get safely to that golden gate; but I was very much afraid for him, the river looked so deep. I looked at the angel who stooped above him in the air with a crown in his hand. No doubt he would soon put it on. Then I read the last few pages, beginning with how the pilgrims reached the land of Beulah, 'where the sun shineth night and day.' What a wonderful river! I supposed it must be a long way off, perhaps not in England at all, and England was a large place; but I thought I should like to find it some day, and did not know that 'some day' I inevitably should.

That night, when Deborah was curling my hair, I said to her, 'Deborah, does Mrs. Wells know you have got that book about the pilgrims?'

'Can't say;' replied Deborah; 'may be she does, may be not.'

I replied, 'Then hadn't you better tell her?'

'Bless the child, why?' said Deborah.

I am not sure that I explained why, or perfectly knew why, but I had an impression that nobody else had such a book, but only Deborah; and probably my remarks made her see this, for I distinctly remember her declaring that Mr. Pipe, the bookseller *down town*, had a great many copies of that very book; that she was sure of it, and that she herself had seen them.

My next question I remember clearly, owing, perhaps, to her making me repeat it several times. It was, 'Have *you* ever seen the wicket gate?'

Deborah stood as if bewildered when I repeated the query. At last, her face suddenly cleared, and she exclaimed, 'Bless the child, I thought she meant the *real thing*, that I did! Yes, my pretty; I've seen it, to be sure, and a very pretty picture it is — Christian just a-going to knock at the door, and ever so many angels looking on. Hold your head still, Miss Rosamond — how the sea air does take your hair out of curl!'

'Then,' said I, 'you have only seen the picture, just the same as I have.'

I do not remember what followed, excepting that, as Deborah clearly had not seen the wicket gate, I began to inquire whether anybody in the neighborhood had seen it, and whether Mr. Pipe had seen it, or had ever been to look for it.

Deborah, to all and each of my questions, replied, that she did not believe anybody had seen it, or had been to look for it; that if anybody knew anything about it, she should judge Mr. Pipe did, for she often saw him reading in his shop as she went by, and everybody said he was a very religious man. Deborah, in answer to my urgent questions, was induced to say that she judged the wicket gate must be a long way off;

and when I inquired whether it was farther off than Dungeness, that is to say, more than ten miles off, she said, 'Yes, it must be a deal farther, I think.' Moreover she drew my curtains, and placed me in bed, and, kissing me, added that I was a little girl, and need not to trouble my head about any wicket gate, nor nothing of the sort; that I should find out what it all meant when I was older; but she could not explain it to me now, as I was not able to understand it.

Children do not lie awake to think of anything, however wonderful. At least I never did, nor did I ever know a child who did, excepting in a book. I fell asleep, and after that two or three mornings passed, during which I was absorbed in my book, and full of wonder as to whether I ought not to go on pilgrimage too. In my exceeding simplicity of mind, I began to save pieces of bread from my meals, and sugar-plums and cake that had been given me, to take with me on the journey; and, as being found quite trustworthy, I was now allowed every day to go out on the beach by myself, or to play in the little belt of wood behind my relative's house. I spent hours in speculating as to whether the lions were not so far off that one could not hear them roar if those waves would leave off surging and splashing among the pebbles; and whether, if I did set out on pilgrimage, Evangelist would be likely to come and show me the way.

One night, while Deborah was again curling my hair, I looked at the red glowing clouds piled up in the glorious west, and reflecting their splendor upon the sea, and I remember certain things that she and I said together. I have no doubt that she had no intention of conveying a false impression to my mind, though she certainly did so ; for I recollect asking her distinctly, whether she thought I might go on a pilgrimage. Whereupon she answered, ' Surely, surely, Miss Rosamond.'

I might, then !

She also told me that the narrow road along which Christian went, and which led to the city of the golden gates, was the road that we all ought to walk in ; and, without at all explaining the allegory, she proceeded to say that it led to heaven.

I went to bed resolved to go on pilgrimage, and when, the next morning, I was told to put on my bonnet and tippet, to go out and play as usual, I took all the pieces of bread that I had saved, and my favorite Dutch doll with a red frock, that I thought I could not part with, and went out.

I went through the garden, and into the little belt of wood. Here I sat down, and began to ponder. Assuredly the wonderful story had said that there was but one way to get to heaven, and that was through the wicket gate. How should I, O, how should I find this wicket gate ! I think that, in my perplexity and fear lest it was my own fault that I could not find the gate, I began to cry ; certainly I have a sort of recollection that my eyes were dazzled and dim, and that when they cleared, some small brown object, which stood at my feet, upon a dwarf fox-glove, suddenly spread open a pair of lovely blue wings. A butterfly ! O, the most beautiful little butterfly in the world ! All thoughts of pilgrimage fled away as it fluttered its wings and floated off to another flower, drawing me after it as surely as many a pretty thing of no higher worth has drawn older hearts from their thoughts of pilgrimage. I ran after it, stopped again and saw it settle, close up, and show me once more those brown wings, mottled with silver, and shaded off into the softest fawn color. I was close to it, and took off my veil, my blue veil, which I always wore, hoping to catch it; but it flew away again; and presently, as I looked, I saw two butterflies instead of one — my beauty had met with a companion — and they were fluttering together towards the great down which lay behind the wood.

To this place I followed, and, running after them over a few yards of short grass, I came to a deep hollow, full of ferns, and edged with camomile, bird's-eye, and dwarf thistles. There, basking in the sun, some hanging to the leaves with folded wings, some spreading them to the light and warmth, I counted blue butterflies by tens and by twenties, and in breathless ecstasy stood considering how I should appropriate some of them, and get them to live happily in my veil, with some flowers, and my splendid Dutch doll, in her red damask gown, for their lady and queen.

About an hour was probably passed in catching a sufficient number for my purpose. It was difficult to do this without hurting them, and as fast as I captured one with my veil others escaped; at last I had about a dozen, and collecting some of the prettiest red and white flowers, and setting my doll among them, I tied up the veil with its own strings, and not doubting that the butterflies must be proud and happy in such a splendid prison, I emerged from the hollow, and set my feet again upon the open down; but this winding hollow was a long one — I had followed it probably for half a mile — and when I came up again there was a green hill between me and the sea, and I did not exactly know where I was; so I turned in the other direction, and I well remember the sudden surprise, amazement I may say, with which I saw one of the commonest sights possible — namely, a narrow path, in which I was standing, and which, with many windings and meanderings, led away over the open grass, and lost itself in the distance among confused outlines of the swelling hills. Could this be the narrow way?

I cannot say that I was satisfied by any means to think that it was, but my mind was filled with childish awe, and I went a little way along it till, casting my eyes not more than half-a-mile before me, I saw, — O, wonderful! almost terrible sight! it was so convincing, and brought the dreamy wonder so near, — I saw, toiling on before me, a man with a burden on his back; a man that now I should call a pedler; but then it *was*, and *could* only be, a pilgrim. So then, this *was* the narrow path; and in the plentitude of my infantine simplicity I wondered whether the people *down town* knew of it; and I went on, still carefully carrying my pretty blue flutterers, for perhaps a mile, when, to my utter confusion, the path branched into three — three distinct paths — and, what was more, the pilgrim whom I was following had descended into a hollow, and had disappeared.

Which of these three paths, then, should I follow? One of them seemed to lead back again towards the town; a second, I thought, was rather too wide and too straight; so I chose the third for my little feet, especially as I thought it was the one in which I had last seen the pedler — I mean the pilgrim — I hope he may have been one.

Not to make my story too long, I wandered about till grass began to be mingled with ferns, and ferns gave place to ling, then in full blosom; at last my path fairly ended, and before me rose a sandy beach, crowned with dwarf oaks, and sprinkled with foxgloves and furze. I had quite lost my way, and my path had been swallowed up in verdure. I was in a great perplexity; and, after climbing to the top of the bank, I looked around and found myself at the brink of a great open place, part down, part heath, intersected with many paths, but no one more like than another to the path that led to the wicket gate. I looked back and saw several better tracks, but could not be sure which was the one I had come by; so large, and so smooth, and so uniform was the waste of grass which, owing to my having attained an elevated spot, was now lying spread before me.

It may have then been about noonday, and I had perhaps been out about three hours; so I was neither tired nor hungry as yet, and kept wandering about in search of the way. At last I saw an elderly gentleman coming towards me on a little pony. He certainly was not a pilgrim; and yet I rejoiced to see him. Mamma had never told me not to look for the wicket gate, therefore, however strange it may appear, I certainly had no consciousness of doing wrong. I had been crying a little before he appeared, not knowing what to do, nor where to turn; and when he approached I was considering what I should say, when he saved me the trouble, and exclaimed, not without a look of surprise, 'Where is your nurse, little girl?'

'Nurse is at home with mamma,' I replied.

'And what are you doing here all by yourself?' he asked.

I replied in all simplicity, 'If you please, I am looking for the wicket gate.'

'The wicket gate! Humph. Well,' shading his eyes and staring around, 'I don't see one. Is it a white gate?'

'I don't know, sir.'

'You don't know! You are a very little girl to be finding your way by yourself in such a place as this. Do you know which side of the heath it is on?'

'No, sir.'

'Well, well,' rejoined my questioner, with great impatience, 'do you know where it leads to?'

'O, yes, sir; it leads to heaven.' Here at least was one question that I could answer; but never shall I forget the face of blank amazement with which he heard me. I was rather frightened at it, and began to explain, in a great hurry, that I had read in the *Pilgrim's Progress* about the wicket gate, and that Deborah had said I might go on pilgrimage; and after this incoherent account I began to cry piteously, and begged the gentleman, if he could not show me the way to the gate, to tell me the way home, because my relative would be so angry, so very angry, if I was late for dinner.

He had descended from his pony, and now asked abruptly, 'How old are you, child?'

'Six years and a half,' I replied, sobbing.

'Six years and a half,' was his not very proper answer, 'and looking out for heaven already!' But being now really alarmed as to whether I should ever find either the gate or my home again, I cried and sobbed heartily, till he sat down on the bank, and taking me on his knee, began to wipe my eyes with his silk pocket-handkerchief, and assure me that he would soon take me home again, for that he knew the way quite well; we were not more than two miles from the beach, and so I need not cry, for we should set off home as soon as I could leave off sobbing.

Thereupon being at ease in my mind, and perfectly satisfied in the good company of the elderly gentleman, he and I 'fell into easy discourse' together. He seemed anxious to investigate this rather strange fancy, and he asked me what I had intended to eat on my pilgrimage. I showed him the various pieces of stale bread and bun that I had saved, and he fell into explosions of loud laughter, which left his face crimson, and his eyes full of tears; but he must have been a very kind elderly gentleman, for he shortly after set me on his little pony, and as he led it homewards over the down, he not only assured me that we should be back in time for dinner, but he took a great deal of pains to impress on my mind that I was never to try to go on pilgrimage again while I was staying at the sea-side, nor afterwards without consulting my mamma. I promised that I would not; and in a very short space of time, as it seemed to me, we came down to the beach, and found ourselves at my relative's gate. Here, as I well remember, my dread of being late induced me to beg my new friend not to leave me till I had ascertained that dinner was not ready; so he left his pony at the gate, and came up to the door. His ring at the bell was soon answered; he explained to the maid that I had lost my way on the downs, and he had brought me home. I was comforted with the assurance that I was just in time for dinner, so I gratefully kissed my new friend, and took leave of him.

Thus ended my first attempt at pilgrimage, leaving nothing behind it but a veil full of blue butterflies. I know it was a childish attempt, but I believe it was sincere; it had something of that faith about it which made the patriarch content long since to 'go forth, not knowing whither he went;' but it was an ignorant faith, and one that would not give up all; it must needs carry a doll with it for comfort and admiration by the way, and it could not help gathering butterflies, things too lovely and too precious, as it seemed, to be passed by. To the follies of our childhood, and for its faults and its short-comings, He will be tender who knows the heart of a child; but if since childhood, setting forth on pilgrimage, we have striven to take with us the goods and the delights of this world; if we have turned back again, lest our friends should be displeased; if we have wavered because any laughed at us, let us pray not only that He 'would forgive us our trespasses,' but that He would ' pardon the iniquity of our holy things.'

THE LIFE OF MR. JOHN SMITH.

THIS great and good man, every event of whose life is well worth preserving, was born in the parish of Cripplegate Within, at half-past ten on Friday, the 1st of April, 1780. He was the only child of his parents, who, perceiving from the first his uncommon sweetness of disposition, and acuteness of intellect, felt a natural pride in watching his progress through infancy.

At seven months he cut his first tooth; at fourteen months he could run alone, and such was his precocity, that, at two years and a half, he could speak his mother tongue sufficiently well to be able to ask for what he wanted.

He began to learn his letters as early as three years old, and soon mastered the whole alphabet, which he would repeat with beautiful precision upon the offer of an apple or a ginger-bread nut.

His father was a brazier, and had a very good business. Jack, as he was then called, was allowed the range of the shop, and possession of all the nails that he could find lying about; thus he soon learned to distinguish between tin tacks, ten-pennies, and brass heads, and having a small hammer of his own, used to amuse himself with knocking them by dozens into a door in the yard, which was soon so thickly studded with them, that you could not see the wood between.

He also had a tin saucepan, which was given him on his seventh birthday by his indulgent father, and in this he often made toffee and hard-bake for his own eating, and thus, while still a mere babe, his mind was turned to philosophical and scientific pursuits; for by means of his nails and hammer he learned the difference between wood and metal, and also the degree of force required to drive the one into the other, whilst with the aid of his saucepan he taught himself many a lesson in the science of eating, — for that it is a science, Soyer has lately demonstrated to the philosophical world.

At seven years old, he being already able to read almost any English book that was placed before him, his father and mother consulted together and resolved to send him to a school at Clapham. There he made such progress as exceeded their most sanguine hopes, and from this school he wrote his first letter, which has been preserved, and runs as follows:—

'DEAR FATHER,— I like school a great deal better than I did at first. My jacket has got two great holes in it, so I am forced to wear my Sunday one. We always have roast beef and Yorkshire *puddin'* for dinner on Sunday, and the boys are very glad of all the nails and screws and nuts I brought with me, and if I might have some more when mother sends my cake and the three pots of jam, and the glue, and the cobbler's wax, and the cabbage-nets, and the packthread, and the fishing-hooks, and the knife, and the new fishing-rod that I asked for when she came to see me, we should all be very glad.

'We have dug a hole in the playground nearly fifteen feet deep, we mean to dig till we get to water, and on half-holidays we fish in the water on the common, where there is an island. The boys want to make a bridge to reach it, but we haven't got anything to make it of. We have not got any fish yet, only newts out of that water, but we saw a good large one on Saturday, and Cooper says he is *determined* he'll have him. Cooper can fish beautifully.

'Dear father, the thieves have stolen all the apples out of the garden, which is a great pity. I send my love to my mother.

'I remain, dear father, your dutiful son,

'JOHN SMITH.'

This interesting letter was read by his parents with tears of joy; indeed, from this time till their son was fifteen years old, he gave them neither trouble nor anxiety, excepting twice — namely, when he took the measles, and when he fought with another boy, and came home with a black eye.

At fifteen, he was apprenticed to his father, and during his apprenticeship his career was as brilliant as could have been desired. Of course he liked to be well dressed, which his mother felt to be the natural consequence of his good looks. He also liked now and then to spend an afternoon in the parks, looking about him, which his father was glad of; for with such powers of observation as he was endowed with it was highly desirable that he should not be without opportunity for exercising them.

At the age of eighteen he had done growing, and measured five feet eight in his shoes; hair brown, with a slight twist in it, scarcely amounting to a curl; complexion moderately fair, and eyes between gray and green. When his apprenticeship was over he paid his addresses to the second daughter of a bookseller in Cheapside, and married her after a three years' courtship. During the next eleven years, Mr. Smith was blessed with seven children—John, his eldest son; Mary, named after her grandmother; Fanny, Thomas, Elizabeth, James, and Sarah.

A few days after the birth of this last, his father died, leaving him the braziery business, and four thousand pounds in the funds. Mr. Smith was a kind son. His mother lived with him, and her old age was cheered by the sight of his honors, worth, and talents. About this time he took out a patent for a new kind of poker; and in the same year his fellow-citizens showed their sense of his deserts by making him an alderman of London.

Happy in the esteem of all, and in the possession of a good business, he lived very quietly till he reached the age of fifty, when his mother died, and was respectably buried by her son in the parish church of Cripplegate.

His eldest son being now able to take charge of the shop and business, Mr. Smith resolved to travel for a month or two. He accordingly went to Ramsgate, where he enjoyed much intellectual pleasure in the prospect of the glorious ocean, and the fine vessels which continually appeared in the offing.

He was a true patriot, and, as he wandered on the beach, in his buff slippers and straw hat, with an umbrella over his head to shield him from the sun, he might often have been heard to sing, with laudable pride, 'Rule Britannia! Britannia rules the waves!'

After sojourning for three weeks at Ramsgate he went northward; nor did he stop till he had reached that city so renowned for its beauty as often to be called the modern Athens—we mean Edinburgh. Mr. Smith wrote home frequently from thence to his family, and made many valuable remarks on the dialect and manners of the inhabitants; but it would appear that he did not altogether approve of what he saw, for in a letter to his son, after praising the goodness of the houses, and the excellence of the gas-fittings, and, indeed, of everything in the iron and brass departments, he observed that the poultry was tough and badly fed, and that the inhabitants had a most unwarrantably high opinion of their city, 'which I can tell you, is as dull compared to London,' he continued, 'as the British Museum is compared with the Pantheon in Oxford Street.' He also, in the same letter, made some new and valuable remarks on the lateness of the season in the North. In proof of the difference between London and Edinburgh he told his son that strawberries were then in full perfection in the latter city, though it was past the middle of August.

Some years after Mr. Smith's return he was elected churchwarden for the parish of Cripplegate, and performed the duties of that situation with great satisfaction to the inhabitants, heading the subscription to the starving Irish with a donation of £5. In the same year he gave £10 to the Middlesex Hospital.

It was not till he reached his sixty-eighth year that Mr. Smith retired from the premises and the sphere he had so long adorned. He then gave up the business to his sons, and retired with his wife to a pleasant residence on Stamford Hill.

He retained his superior faculties to the last; for, at the time when there was so much stir about the Nineveh Marbles, he went, though very infirm, to see them, and, with his usual sound sense, remarked that they did not answer his expectations: as there was so much marble in the country, and also Derbyshire spar, he wondered that Government had not new articles manufactured, instead of sending abroad for old things which were cracked already.

At the age of seventy Mr. Smith died, universally respected, and was buried in the cemetery at Kensall Green.

'And is this all?' cries the indignant reader.

All? I am amazed at your asking such a question! I should have thought you had had enough of it! Yes, it *is* all; and to tell you a secret, which, of course, I would not proclaim to the world, I should not be in the least surprised if *your* biography, up to the present date, is not one bit better worth writing.

What have *you* done, I should like to know? and what are you, and what have you been, that is better worth recording than the sayings and doings recorded here? You think yourself superior? Well, you *may be*, certainly; and to reflect that you *are*, is a comfortable thing for yourself. And notwithstanding that I say this, I have a true regard for you, and am far from forgetting that though the events of your life may never be striking, or worth recording, the tenor of your life may be useful and happy, and the record may be written on high. In conclusion, however, I cannot forbear telling you that, whether you are destined to be great or little, the honor of writing your biography is not desired by your obedient servant the biographer of Mr. John Smith.

THE LONELY ROCK.

THE LONELY ROCK.

THREE summers ago I had a severe illness, and on recovering from it, my father took me for change of air, not to one of our pretty townish watering-places, but up to the very North of Scotland, to a place which he had himself delighted in when a boy, a lonely farm-house, standing on the shore of a rocky bay in one of the Orkneys.

My father is a Highlander, and though he has lived in England from his early youth, he retains, not only a strong love for his own country, but a belief in its healthfulness; he is fond of indulging the fancy that scenery which the fathers have delighted in, will not strike on the senses of the children as something new and strange, but they will enter the hereditary region with a half-formed notion that they must have seen it before, and it will possess a soothing power over them which is better than familiarity itself.

I had often heard my father express this idea, but had neither understood nor believed in it. The listlessness of illness made me indifferent as to what became of me, and during our steam voyage I cared neither to move nor to look about me. But the result proved that my father was right. It was dark when we reached our destination, but I no sooner opened my eyes the next morning than a delightful home-feeling came over me; I could not look about me enough, and yet nothing was sufficiently unexpected to cause me the least surprise.

It was August, the finest part of the northern summer; and as I lay on pillows, looking out across the bay, I enjoyed that perfect quietude and peace so grateful to those who have lately suffered from the turmoil and restlessness of fever. I had imagined myself always surrounded by shifting, hurrying crowds, always oppressed by the gaze of unbidden guests; how complete and welcome was this change, this seclusion! No one but my father and the young servant whom we had brought with us could speak a word that I understood, and I could fall asleep and wake again, quite secure from the slightest interruption.

By the first blush of dawn I used to wake up, and lie watching that quiet bay; there would be the shady crags, dark and rocky, lifting and stretching themselves as if to protect and embrace the water, which, perhaps, would be lying utterly still, or just lapping against them, and softly swaying to and fro the long banners of seaweed which floated out from them.

Or, perhaps, a thin mist would be hanging across the entrance of the bay, like a curtain drawn from cliff to cliff; presently this snowy curtain would turn of an amber color, and glow towards the centre; once I wondered if that sudden glow could be a ship on fire, and watched it in fear; but I soon saw the gigantic sun thrust himself up, so near, as it seemed, that the farthest cliffs as they melted into the mist appeared farther off than he — so near, that it was surprising to count the number of little fishing-boats that crossed between me and his great disk; still more surprising to watch how fast he receded, growing so refulgent that he dazzled my eyes, while the mist began to waver up and down, curl itself, and roll away to sea, till on a sudden up sprang a little breeze, and the water, which had been white, streaked here and there with a line of yellow, was blue almost before I could mark the change, and covered with brisk little ripples, and the mist had melted back into some half-dozen caverns, within which it soon receded and was lost.

I used to lie and learn that beautiful bay by heart. In the afternoon the water was often of a pale sea-green, and the precipitous cliffs were speckled with multitudes of sea-birds; and bright in the sunshine I loved to watch at a distance the small mountain goats climbing from point to point; wherever there was a strip of grass I was sure to see their white breasts; but above all things, I loved to watch the long wavy reflection of a tall black rock which was perfectly isolated, and stood out to sea in the very centre of the bay. I was the more occupied in fancy with this rock, because, unlike the other features of the landscape, it never changed.

The sea was white, it was yellow, it was green, it was blue; the sea was gone a long way off, and the sands were bare; the sea was come back again, was rushing between every little rock, and powdering the tops of them with spray; the sea was clear as a mirror, and white gulls were swimming on it by thousands; the sea was restless, and the rocking boats were tossing up and down on it. And the cliffs? In moonlight they were castles, and they were ships; in sunshine they were black, brown, blue, green, and ruddy, according to the clouds and the height of the sun. Their shadows, too, now a narrow strip at their bases, now an overshadowing mass, gave endless variety to the scene.

But this one black rock out at sea never seemed to change. In appearance at that distance it was a massive column, square, and bending inward at the centre, so as to make it lean towards the northern shore. Considering this changeless character, it was rather strange that in my dreams, still vivid from recent illness, this column always assumed the likeness of a man. A stern man it seemed to be, with head sunk on his breast, and arms gathered under the folds of a dark heavy mantle; yet when I awoke and looked out over the bay, the blue moonbeams would not drop on my rock, or its reflection, in such a way as to make it any other than the bare, bleak, bending thing that I always saw it.

In a week I was able to come out of doors, and wander by the help of my father's arm along the strip of yellow sand by the sea. How delightful was the feeling of leaf, pebble, sand, or seaweed to my hand, which so long had been used to nothing but the soft linen of my pillow! How beautiful and fresh everything looked out of doors! how delicious was the sound of the little inch-deep waves as they ran and spread briskly out over the flat green floors of the caverns! how still more delicious the crisp rustling of the displaced pebbles, when these capricious waves receded!

And the caverns! How I stood looking into them, sunny and warm as they were at the entrance, and gloomily grand within! What a pleasure it was to think that the world should be so full of beautiful places, even where few had cared to look at them! how wonderful to think that the self-same echo, which answered my voice when I sang to it, was always lying there ready to be spoken with, though rarely invoked but by the winds and the waves; that ever since the Deluge, perhaps, it had possessed this power to mock human utterance, but unless it had caught up and repeated the cries of some drowning fisher-boy, or shipwrecked mariner, and sent them back again more wild than before, its mocking syllables and marvellous cadences had never been tested but by me!

And the first sail in a boat was a pleasure which can never be forgotten.

It was a still afternoon when we stepped into that boat — so still that we had oars as well as the flapping sail; I had wished to row out to sea as far as the rock, and now I was to have my wish. On and on we went, looking by turns into the various clefts and caverns; at last we stood out into the middle of the bay, and very soon we had left the cliffs altogether behind. We were out in the open sea, but still the rock was far before us; it became taller, larger, and more important, but yet it presented the same outline, and precisely the same aspect, when, after another half-hour's rowing, we drew near it, and I could hear the water lapping against its inhospitable sides.

The men rested on their oars, and allowed the boat to drift down towards it. There it stood, high, lonely, inaccessible. I looked up; there was scarcely a crevice where a sea-fowl could have built, not a level slip large enough for human foot to stand upon, nor projection for hand of drowning man to seize on.

Shipwreck and death it had often caused, it was the dread and scourge of the bay, but it yielded no shelter nor food for beast or bird; not a blade of grass waved there — nothing stood there.

We rowed several times round it, and every moment I became more impressed with its peculiar character and situation, so completely aloof from everything else — even another rock as hard and black as itself, standing near it, would have been apparent companionship. If one goat had fed there, if one sea-bird had nestled there, if one rope of tangled seaweed had rooted there, and floated out on the surging water to meet the swimmer's hand — but no; I looked, and there was not one. The water washed up against it, and it flung back the water; the wind blew against it, and it would not echo the wind; its very shadow was useless, for it dropped upon nothing that wanted shade. By day the fisherman looked at it only to steer clear of it, and by night, if he struck against it, he went down. Hard, dreary, bleak! I looked at it as we floated slowly towards home; there it stood rearing up its desolate head, a forcible image, and a true one, of a thoroughly selfish, a thoroughly unfeeling and isolated, human heart.

Now let us go back a long time, and talk about

things which happened before we were born. I do not mean centuries ago, when the sea-kings, in their voyages plundering that coast, drove by night upon the rock and went down. *That* is not the long time ago of which I want to speak; nor of that other long time ago, when two whaling vessels, large and deeply laden, bounded against it in a storm, and beat up against it till the raging waves tore them to pieces, and splitting and grinding every beam and spar, scarcely threw one piece of wreck on the shore which was as long as the bodies of the mariners. I am not going to tell of the many fishing-boats which went out and were seen no more — of the many brave men that hard by that fatal place went under the surging water, of the many toiling rowers that made, as they thought, straight for home, and struck, and had only time for one cry — 'The Rock! the Rock!' The long time ago, of which I mean to tell, was a wild night in March, during which, in a fisherman's hut ashore, sat a young girl at her spinning-wheel, and looked out on the dark driving clouds, and listened, trembling, to the wind and the sea.

The morning light dawned at last. One boat that should have been riding on the troubled waves was missing — her father's boat! and half a mile from his cottage, her father's body was washed up on the shore.

This happened fifty years ago, and fifty years is a long time in the life of a human being; fifty years is a long time to go on in such a course, as the woman did of whom I am speaking. She watched her father's body, according to the custom of her people, till he was laid in the grave. Then she lay down on her bed and slept, and by night got up and set a candle in her casement, as a beacon to the fishermen and a guide. She sat by the candle all night, and trimmed it, and spun; then when day dawned she went to bed and slept in the sunshine.

So many hanks as she had spun before for her daily bread, she spun still, and one over, to buy her nightly candle; and from that time to this, for fifty years, through youth, maturity, and old age, she has turned night into day, and in the snow-storms of winter, through driving mists, deceptive moonlight, and solemn darkness, that northern harbor has never once been without the light of her candle.

How many lives she saved by this candle, or how many a meal she won by it for the starving families of the boatmen, it is impossible to say; how many a dark night the fishermen, depending on it, went fearlessly forth, cannot now be told. There it stood, regular as a light-house, steady as constant care could make it. Always brighter when daylight waned, they had only to keep it constantly in view and they were safe; there was but one thing that could intercept it, and that was the Rock. However far they might have stretched out to sea, they had only to bear down straight for that lighted window, and they were sure of a safe entrance into the harbor.

Fifty years of life and labor — fifty years of sleeping in the sunshine — fifty years of watching and self-denial, and all to feed the flame and trim the wick of that one candle! But if we look upon the recorded lives of great men, and just men, and wise men, few of them can show fifty years of worthier, certainly not of more successful labor. Little, indeed, of the 'midnight oil' consumed during the last half century so worthily deserved the trimming. Happy woman — and but for the dreaded rock her great charity might never have been called into exercise!

But what do the boatmen and the boatmen's wives think of this? Do they *pay* the woman?

No; they are very poor; but poor or rich, they know better than that.

Do they thank her?

No. Perhaps they feel that thanks of theirs would be inadequate to express their obligations, or, perhaps, long years have made the lighted casement so familiar, that they look on it as a matter of course.

Sometimes the fishermen lay fish on her threshold, and set a child to watch it for her till she wakes; sometimes their wives steal into her cottage, now she is getting old, and spin a hank or two of thread for her while she slumbers; and they teach their children to pass her hut quietly, and not to sing and shout before her door, lest they should disturb her. That is all. Their thanks are not looked for — scarcely supposed to be due. Their grateful deeds are more than she expects, and as much as she desires.

How often, in the far distance of my English home, I have awoke in a wild winter night, and while the wind and storm were rising, have thought of that northern bay, with the waves dashing against the rock, and have pictured to myself the casement, and the candle nursed by that bending, aged figure! How delightful to know that through her untiring charity the rock has long lost more than half its terrors, and to consider that, curse though it may be to all besides, it has most surely proved a blessing to her!

You, too, may perhaps think with advantage on the character of this woman, and contrast it with the mission of the Rock. There are many degrees between them. Few, like the rock, stand up wholly to work ruin and destruction; few, like the woman, 'let their light shine' so brightly for good. But to one of the many degrees between them we must all most certainly belong — we all lean towards the woman or the rock. On such characters you do well to speculate with me, for you have not been cheated into sympathy with ideal shipwreck or imaginary kindness. There is many a rock elsewhere as perilous as the one I have told you of — perhaps there are many such women; but for this one, whose story is before you, pray that her candle may burn a little longer, since this record of her charity is true.

CAN AND COULD.

ONCE upon a time, Could went out to take a walk on a winterly morning; he was very much out of spirits, and he was made more so by the necessity under which he found himself to be frequently repeating his own name. 'O, if I could,' and 'O that I were rich and great, for then I could do so and so.'

About the tenth time that he said this, Can opened the door of her small house, and set out on an errand. She went down a back street and through a poor neighborhood; she was not at all a grand personage, not nearly so well dressed, or lodged, or educated, as Could; and, in fact, was altogether more humble, both in her own esteem and that of others. She opened her door and went down the street, neither sauntering nor looking about her, for she was in a hurry.

All on a sudden, however, this busy little Can stopped and picked up a piece of orange peel. 'A dangerous trick,' she observed, 'to throw orange peel about, particularly in frosty weather, and in such a crowded thoroughfare;' and she bustled on till she overtook a tribe of little children who were scattering it very freely; they had been bargaining for oranges at an open fruit stall, and were eating them as they went along. 'Well, it's little enough that I have in my power,' thought Can, 'but certainly I can speak to these children, and try to persuade them to leave off strewing orange peel.

Can stopped. 'That's a pretty baby that you have in your arms,' she said to one of them; 'how old is he.'

'He's fourteen months old,' answered the small nurse, 'and he begins to walk; I teach him, he's my brother.'

'Poor little fellow,' said Can, 'I hope you are kind to him; you know if you were to let him fall he might never be able to walk any more.'

'I never let him drop,' replied the child, 'I always take care of my baby.'

'And so do I;' 'And so do I,' repeated other shrill voices, and two more babies were thrust up for Can's inspection.

'But if you were to slip down yourselves on this hard pavement you would be hurt, and the baby would be hurt in your arms. Look! how can you be so careless as to throw all this peel about; don't you know how slippery it is?'

'We always fling it down,' said one.

'And I never slipped down but once on a piece,' remarked another.

'But was not that once too often?'

'Yes; I grazed my arm very badly, and broke a cup that I was carrying.'

'Well, now, suppose you pick up all the peel you can find; and then go down the streets round about and see how much you can get; and to the one who finds most, when I come back, I shall give a penny.'

So after making the children promise that they would never commit this fault again, Can went on; and it is a remarkable circumstance, that just at that very moment, as Could was walking in quite a different part of London, he also came to a piece of orange peel which was lying across his path.

'What a shame!' he said, as he passed on; 'what a disgrace it is to the city authorities, that this practice of sowing seed, which springs up into broken bones, cannot be made a punishable offence; there is never a winter that one or more accidents do not arise from it! If I could only put it down, how glad I should be! If, for instance, I could offer a bribe to people to abstain from it; or if I could warn or punish; or if I could be placed in a position to legislate for the suppression of this and similar bad habits. But, alas! my wishes rise far above my powers; my philanthropic aspirations can find no —'

'By your leave,' said a tall strong man, with a heavy coal sack on his shoulders.

Could, stepping aside, permitted the coal porter to pass him. 'Yes,' he continued, taking up his soliloquy where it had been interrupted, 'it is strange that so many anxious wishes for the welfare of his species should be implanted in the breast of a man who has no means of gratifying them.' The noise of a thundering fall, and the rushing down as of a great shower of stones, made Could turn hastily round. Several people were running together, they stooped over something on the ground, it was the porter; he had fallen on the pavement, and the coals lay in heaps about his head; some people were clearing them away, others were trying to raise him. Could advanced and saw that the man was stunned, for he looked about him with a bewildered expression, and talked incoherently. Could also observed that a piece of orange peel was adhering to the sole of his shoe.

'How sad!' said Could; 'now, here is the bitter result of this abuse. If I had been in authority I could have prevented this; how it chafes the spirit to perceive, and be powerless! Poor fellow! he is evidently stunned, and has a broken limb — he is lamed, perhaps for life. People are certainly very active and kind on these occasions: they seem preparing to take him to the hospital. Such an accident as this is enough to make a man wish he could be a king or a lawgiver; what the poet says may be true enough: —

"Of all the ills that human kind endure,
Small is that part which laws can cause or cure."

And yet I think I could have framed such a law, that this poor fellow might now have been going about his work, instead of being carried to languish for weeks on a sick bed, while his poor family are half starved, and must perhaps receive him at last, a peevish, broken-spirited cripple, a burden for life, instead of a support; and all because of a pitiful piece of scattered orange peel!'

While Could was still moralizing thus, he got into an omnibus, and soon found himself drawing near one of the suburbs of London, turning and winding among rows of new houses with heaps of bricks before them, and the smell of mortar in their neighborhood; then among railway excavations and embankments, and at last among neat villas and cottages standing in gardens, with here and there a field behind them. Presently they passed a large building, and Could read upon its front, 'Temporary Home for Consumptive Patients.' 'An excellent institution,' he thought to himself; 'here a poor man or woman can have a few weeks of good air, good food, and good nursing, the best things possible for setting them up, at least for a time. I have often thought that these remedial institutions do more good, on the whole, than mere hospitals; and, if I could afford it, I would rather be the founder of one of them than of places with more ambitious aims and names. It is sad to think how much consumption is on the increase among the poor; bad air, and the heated places where so many of them work, give these winterly blasts a terrible power over them. But it is my lot to sigh over their troubles without being able to soften them. A small competence, a fixed income, which does no more than provide for my own wants, and procure those simple comforts and relaxations which are necessary to me, is of all things least favorable for the realizing of my aspirations. I cannot gratify my benevolent wishes, though their constant presence shows how willingly I would if I could.'

The omnibus stopped, and a man, in clean working clothes, inquired whether there was an inside place.

'No, there is not one,' said the conductor, and he looked in; most of the passengers were women.

'Would any gentleman like to go outside?'

'Like!' thought Could with a laugh; 'who would like in such a wind as this, so searching and wild? Thank Heaven, I never take cold; but I don't want a blast like this to air the lining of my paletôt, make itself acquainted with the pattern of my handkerchief, and chill the very shillings in my waistcoat pocket.'

'Because,' continued the conductor, 'if any gentleman would like to go outside, here is a person who has been ill, and would be very glad of a place within.'

He looked down, as he spoke, upon the man, whose clothes were not well calculated to defend him against the weather, and who looked sickly, and had a hollow cough. No answer came from within.

'I must get outside, then,' said the man, 'for I have not much time for waiting,' so he mounted, and the driver spread part of his own wrapper over his legs, another passenger having lent a hand to help him up.

'Thank you, sir,' said the man; 'I am but weak; but I am sorry to give you the trouble.'

'No trouble, no trouble,' answered the outside passenger; and he muttered to himself, 'You are not likely to trouble any one long.'

'That's where you come from, I suppose,' said the driver, pointing with his whip towards the house for consumptive patients.

'Yes,' said the man, 'I have been very ill indeed; but I am better now, wonderfully better. They say I may last for years with proper attention, and they tell me to be very careful of weather; but what can I do?'

CAN AND COULD.

'It's very cold and windy for you up here,' said the driver.

The man shivered, but did not complain; he looked about him with a bright glitter in his eyes, and every time he coughed he declared that he was much better than he had been.

After telling you so much about Could, his kind wishes, projects, and aspirations, I am almost ashamed to mention Can to you again; however, I think I will venture, though her aspirations, poor little thing, are very humble ones, and she scarcely knows what a project means.

So, you must know that having concluded most of her business, she entered a shop to purchase something for her dinner; and while she waited to be served a child entered, carrying a basket much too heavy for her strength, and having a shawl folded up on her arm.

'What have you in your basket?' asked Can.

'Potatoes for dinner,' said the child.

'It's very heavy for you,' remarked Can, observing how she bent under the weight of it.

'Mother's ill, and there's nobody to go to the shop but me,' replied the child, setting it down, and blowing her numbed fingers.

'No wonder you are cold,' said Can; 'why don't you put your shawl on instead of carrying it so?'

'It's so big,' said the child, in a piteous voice. 'Mother put a pin in it, and told me to hold it up; but I can't, the basket's so heavy, and I trod on it and fell down.'

'It's enough to give the child her death of cold,'

said the mistress of the shop, 'to go crawling home in this bitter wind, with nothing on but that thin frock.'

'Come,' said Can, 'I'm not very clever, but, at least, I know how to tie a child's shawl so as not to throw her down.' So she made the little girl hold out her arms, and drawing the garment closely round her, knotted it securely at her back. 'Now, then,' she said, having inquired where she lived, 'I am going your way, so I can help you to carry your basket."

Can and the child then went out together, while Could, having reached his comfortable home, sat down before the fire and made a great many reflections; he made reflections on baths and wash-houses, and wished he could advance their interests; he made reflections on model prisons and penitentiaries, and wished he could improve them; he made reflections on the progress of civilization, on the necessity for some better mode of educating the masses; he thought of the progress of the human mind, and made grand projects in his benevolent head whereby all the true interests of the race might be advanced, and he wished he could carry them into practice; he reflected on poverty, and made castles in the air as to how he might mitigate its severity, and then having in imagination made many people happy, he felt that a benevolent disposition was a great blessing, and fell asleep over the fire.

Can only made two things. When she had helped to carry the child's basket, she kindly made her sick mother's bed, and then she went home and made a pudding.

THE SUSPICIOUS JACKDAW.

THERE never was a more suspicious mortal in this world than old Madam Mortimer, unless it was Madam Mortimer's Jackdaw. To see him peep about, and turn his head on one side as if to listen, and go and stand on the edge of her desk with his bright eye fixed on her letters, and then flutter to her wardrobe, and peer behind her cabinets, as if he suspected that in cracks and crevices, under tables and behind screens, there must be other daws hidden, who would interfere with his particular interests, or listen to the remarks made to him when he and his mistress were alone, or find the bits of crust that he had stowed away for his own eating; to see all this, I say, was quite as good amusement as to see old Madam Mortimer occupying herself in the same way, indeed quite in the same way, considering the different natures of women and jackdaws.

Sometimes Madam Mortimer would steal up softly to her door, and turn the handle very softly in her hand; then she would open it just by a little crack and listen till she must have had the ear-ache; but generally after this exercise, she would return to her seat, saying aloud, as she took up her knitting, 'Well, I declare, I thought that was the butcher's boy talking to cook; an idle young fellow, that he is; brings all the gossip of the village here, I'm certain. However, this once I'm wrong; it's only gardener sitting outside the scullery, helping her to shell peas. He had better be doing that than doing nothing — which is what most of his time is passed in, I suspect.'

Here the jackdaw would give a little croak, to express his approval of the sentiment; whenever his mistress finished a speech, he made a point of either croaking or coughing, just like a human being. The foot-boy had taught him this accomplishment, and his mistress could never help laughing when she heard him cough. No more could little Patience Grey, who was Madam Mortimer's maid. She was very young, only fourteen, but then Madam Mortimer suspected that if she had an older maid she should have more trouble in keeping her in order; so she took Patience from school to wait on her, and Patience was very happy in the great old silent house, with its long oaken galleries; and as there really seemed to be nothing about her for either Madam Mortimer's or the jackdaw's suspicion to rest upon, she was very seldom scolded, though sometimes when she came into the parlor, looking rather hot and breathing quickly, her mistress would alarm her by saying, 'Patience, you've been skipping in the yard. You need not deny it, for I know you have.'

Here Patience would answer, blushing, — 'I just skipped for a few minutes, ma'am, after I had done plaiting your frills.' 'Ah, you'll never be a woman,'

Mrs. Mortimer would answer, 'never! if you live to be a hundred.' And it did not enter into the head of little Patience that her mistress could see everything that was done in the yard, and how she sometimes ran and played with the house dog under the walnut-trees, the two old walnut-trees that grew there; and how she played at ball in the coach-house, when she had finished all her needlework, while the little dog, and the big dog, and the big dog's two puppies, sat watching at the open door, ready to rush in and seize the ball if she let it drop. It never entered into her giddy head that her mistress could see all this, for her mistress sat in a large upper parlor, and through one of its windows overlooked the yard; the blind was always drawn down, and how could Patience suppose that her mistress could peep through a tiny hole in it, and that she did this continually, so that not a postman could politely offer an orange to the housemaid, nor she in return reward him with a mug of beer, without being seen by the keen eyes of Madame Mortimer!

Patience, on the whole, however, fared none the worse for being watched — quite the contrary; the more the jackdaw and his mistress watched her, the fonder they grew. She was such a guileless little maid, that they liked to have her in the large old parlor with them, helping Madam Mortimer with her needlework, and letting the jackdaw peep into her work-box. One day, when Patience was sent for to attend her mistress, she found her with the contents of an old cabinet spread open before her; there were corals with silver bells, there were old silver brooches, and there were many rings and necklaces, and old-fashioned ornaments that

Patience thought extremely handsome; in particular, there was a cornelian necklace, made of cut cornelians, which she considered to be particularly beautiful; so did the jackdaw, for when Madam Mortimer allowed Patience to wash this necklace in some warm water, he stood on the edge of the basin pecking at it playfully, as if he wanted to get it from her. Patience would not let him have it, and when she had carefully dried it she laid it on some clean cotton wool, and said to the jackdaw, 'You are not going to have it, Jack. It's the most beautiful thing that mistress has got, so I reckon she'll never let you touch it.'

When Madam Mortimer heard this, she smiled covertly at the ignorance of Patience, and presently said to her, 'Child, you may go down and ask for a piece of leather and some rouge powder, and I will show you how to clean this set of emeralds.'

So Patience ran down to the footboy, and got what she required, and very happy she was under her mistress's directions in polishing and cleaning the jewels — quite as happy as she could have felt if they had been her own; yet, when Madam Mortimer said to her, 'Which do you think the handsomest now, Patience; the green stones or the red ones?' she replied, 'O, the red ones are the handsomest, ma'am, by a deal.'

Just at this moment visitors were announced, and Madam Mortimer retired to her own room previous to seeing them, taking Patience with her to attend on her, and see to the set of her lace shawl, and of a new cap that she donned for the occasion. She turned the key of the parlor where all her jewelry lay about, and the jackdaw, as he hopped with her out of the room, coughed approvingly of the deed, in a manner as expressive as if he had said, 'Who knows whether all the people about us are honest?'

The old lady put the key into her basket, but, strange to say, she forgot her basket, and left that in her bedroom with Patience, while she went down to receive her visitors; and all that evening, suspicious as she generally was, she never once remembered that any one could unlock the parlor-door by means of this basket; on the contrary, she was in very good spirits, and she and her elder visitor talked nearly all the evening about their servants, and about what a trouble servants were, while the younger ladies walked in the garden, gathered a few flowers, and partook of some strawberries.

Now Madam Mortimer, suspicious though she was, had an exceedingly kind heart, and she very often allowed the housemaid to attend on her at night, that Patience might go to bed early, as befitted her age. The visitors staid late, but at nine the drawing-room bell was rung, and orders were sent out that Patience was to go to bed; so as it was the full of the midsummer moon, she stole upstairs without a candle, and when alone in her little garret it was quite light enough for her to examine various little treasures that she kept in her box. She was busy so doing, when Jack flew in at the open window, and lighted on her feet as she knelt, then fluttered on to her shoulder, and peeped down at her treasures, and began to make a great croaking and chattering. Patience thought he was more than usually inquisitive that night, and I am afraid he somewhat interfered with her attention while she was reading her chapter, for he would not let her pincushion alone, but would persist in pulling out the pins, and dropping them on to the floor, listening with his head on one side to the slight noise they made when they fell. At last he flew out at the window. And what did he do next?

Why, he did not go to roost, as he would have done if he had not been for so many years accustomed to civilized society, but he flew once or twice round the house to see that other birds were asleep, and not likely to watch his movements, and then he peeped down the chimneys, where the swallows, now rearing their second broods, sat fast asleep on the nest; he next alighted on the roof, and walked cautiously to a certain crevice, where he kept a few dozens of nails, that he had picked with his beak out of the carpet, and a good many odds and ends of ribbon, bits of worsted, farthings, and broken morsels of crockery, that he valued highly; these he pulled out of the crevice, and then he poked his property with his beak, chattered to it in a very senseless way, walked over it, and finally deposited it again in the crevice, flew down to the side of the house, and entered the parlor where his mistress's jewelry lay.

Here lay the necklace — it looked very pretty — the jackdaw alighted on the table, pecked it as thinking that it might be good to eat, then lifted it up and shook it. At last he flew with it out of the window.

It was still quite light out of doors, and as the necklace dangled from his beak, he admired it very much. 'But what did he want with it?' you will naturally ask.

Nobody knows, but this is ascertained — that, finding it heavy, he took it, not to the roof, but to the edge of a deep well in the garden, wherein he had deposited the cook's brass thimble, and several of her skewers; having reached this well, and lighted on the stone brink, he peered down into it, and saw his own image, and the red necklace in his beak; he also saw four or five little stars reflected there, and as it was his bedtime, he dozed a little on the edge of the well, while the evening air waved slightly the long leaves of the ferns that hung over it, and grew in the joints of the stone many feet down.

At last, it is supposed that some such thought as this crossed his brain: 'These berries are heavy, and not good to eat; I had better lay them on the water till to-morrow morning.'

So he let them drop, and down they fell to the bottom. He had dropped a good many articles before this into the well; some, such as nuts, feathers, and bits of stick and straw, floated; others, like this necklace, had sunk. It was all chance which happened, but he liked to hear the splash of the red necklace, and he stood awhile chattering to himself, with great serenity of mind, on the occasion of its disappearing; then he went and pecked at the kitchen window, demanding his supper.

This is what the jackdaw did; and now what did the mistress do, when she walked to the parlor door the next morning, unlocked it, and found that the red necklace was gone?

She was quite amazed — nobody but Patience could have taken it — little Patience, her good little maid, who had seemed so guileless, so conscientious, and so honest. O, what a sad thing it was that there was nobody in the world that she could trust! Patience must have taken the key, and after using it for this bad purpose, must have placed it again in the basket.

But Madam Mortimer was so sorry to think of this, that she decided to let Patience have a little time to reflect upon her great fault and confess it. So she said nothing to her all the morning, and in the afternoon, peeping through her little hole in the blind, she saw Patience chasing the ducks into the pond, and laughing heartily to see them plunge. 'Hardened child,' said her mistress, 'how can she laugh?—I'll give her warning;' and thereupon she sat down in her easy chair and began to cry. Now, she felt, almost for the first time, what a sad thing it is to suspect a person whom one really loves. She had not supposed how much she cared for this little village girl till she was obliged to suspect her. She had not perceived how sad her constant habit of suspicion was, and how it had now obtained such a dominion over her, till everything done by a suspected person appeared to her mind in a distorted light. Now the childish simplicity of Patience seemed to her to be hardened guilt. Now, when she saw her at play, she made up her mind that the little girl knew she was overlooked, and was playing about in order to make her mistress think she was at ease, and had nothing weighing on her spirits; and when she came into the parlor, if she was awkward, her mistress attributed it to guilty fears; and if she made any mistake about a message, it was because her thoughts were pre-occupied with her ill-gotten trinket.

This unhappy state of things went on for several days. At last, one evening, Madam Mortimer happening to look out at her hole in the blind, saw Patience slowly walking across the yard, and cautiously looking down into her apron, which she had gathered up into her hands. Madam Mortimer felt convinced that the poor child had got the necklace concealed there. One of the housemaids came up, but Patience ran away, and would not let her see what she had got, and seemed so anxious to conceal it, that her mistress drew up the blind, opened the window, and said, in an awful voice, 'Patience, come here!' The little girl approached — there was a veranda outside the window, and some wooden steps led up to it. 'Come up to me,' said her mistress. The little girl said, 'Yes, ma'am;' and still holding her apron, turned to enter the door. 'No,' exclaimed her mistress; 'come up these steps; I do not want to lose sight of you.' Patience obeyed. Her mistress sat down, and the little maid stood opposite to her.

'Patience,' said her mistress, 'I have lost my red necklace.' The little girl glanced under the table, as if she thought the necklace might have dropped there.

'Do you know where it is, Patience?' was the next question, asked with great solemnity. Patience tightened the folds of her apron, looked earnestly at her mistress, and said, 'No, ma'am.'

'Poor child,' replied Madam Mortimer shaking her head; and Patience, not appearing to know what she meant, colored exceedingly, and looked as if she was going to cry. But at last, as her mistress sat in her chair, and did not say another word, she began to steal away till she was arrested by her mistress's voice.

'Come back again, you poor misguided child — come back, and show me what you have got in your apron.' As Madame Mortimer spoke she started, for the evening was growing dusk, and when Patience turned, a light, a decided light, gleamed through her white apron.

'Please, ma'am,' she said, now holding it open, 'it's some glow-worms that old gardener gave me — three glow-worms, and some leaves that I got for them.'

'Bless me!' exclaimed Madam Mortimer, when she saw the shining insects slowly moving about on her little maid's apron; but she looked so much less angry than before, that Patience, by way of peace-offering, took up one of her treasures, and placed it, with some leaves, upon the open page of her mistress's great Bible, which lay on a little table by her side.

'You may go, now, Patience,' said her mistress, quite calmly, and the little girl left the room, while her mistress sat so long, lost in thought, that it grew quite dusk. 'After all,' she thought, 'that poor child must have been the thief; nobody else could have stolen the necklace; but I will still give her time to confess and restore it.' As she said this she turned towards the Bible, and the glow-worm on the page was slowly moving along it; the darkness hid every other word, but she read by the light of her little maid's gift, as it went on, this verse: 'We — do — all — fade — as — doth — a — leaf.'

'Too true,' said the poor old lady, sighing, 'I feel the coming on of old age very fast, and I could have wished to have somebody about me, however young, that I could trust. Ah, we are frail creatures — we come up and die down like the summer grass; and we are as sinful as we are frail. My poor little Patience! I will try her a little longer.' So saying, the mistress began to doze, and the jackdaw hopped down from the perch where he had been watching her, and when he saw that she was fast asleep, and that the yellow moonlight was soft upon her aged features, he alighted on the page of the Bible which the shining glow-worm was then illuminating, and pounced upon him and ate him up.

Little Patience carried her glow-worms upstairs, and amused herself with them a long time; for she had nothing to do but to enjoy herself when her daily task of needlework was done; and as her mistress never set her more to accomplish than she could finish before dusk, she often had a good game at play with a clear conscience. That night, however, she was not in such good spirits as usual, because her mistress had been angry with her, and if it had not been for the glow-worms she would have felt very dull indeed.

However, she hung them up in a gauze bag that she had made for them, and long after she was in bed she lay looking at them, but thought they grew brighter and brighter. She fell fast asleep at last, and fast asleep she was when her mistress came into the room with a candle in her hand, and softly stole up to her bedside.

Patience looked very happy and peaceful in her sleep, and the suspicious old lady could find nothing lying about to excite her doubts. The child had left her box open, and Madam Mortimer, though she did not choose to touch or move anything in it, used her eyes very sharply, and scrutinized its contents with astonishing deliberation. At length Patience moved, and Madam Mortimer, shading her candle, stole away again, feeling that she had done something to be ashamed of.

The next morning she sent for Patience, and said to her, 'Patience, I told you that I had lost my red necklace; I must have you to help me to search for it; but first tell me whether you know where it is?'

'I know where I think it is, ma'am,' Patience answered quite simply.

'Where?' asked her mistress; but she spoke and looked so severely that Patience hung her head and faltered, and at last said, 'She didn't know, she only thought it might be;' and when pressed for an answer, she said, 'She thought it might be in the empty side of the tea-caddy, for Jack often took things and put them into it.' While the little girl spoke she looked so bashful and confused, that her mistress was confirmed in her bad opinion of her; but she allowed her to help all the morning in searching for the lost necklace; 'for, after all,' she thought, 'I *may* be mistaken.'

However, the necklace was not to be found; and though the jackdaw chattered and bustled about a great deal, and told over and over again, in the jackdaw's language, what he had done with it, nobody took the slightest notice of him; and the longer she searched, the more unhappy Madam Mortimer became. 'It is not the value of the necklace,' she often said to herself; 'but it is the being obliged to suspect this child, that I am so sorry for; for she was the only person in the wide world that I felt I could trust, excepting my own children.'

But if people trust *only* one person, and can make up their minds to be distrustful of every one else, their suspicions are almost sure at last to reach the one remaining; and so Madam Mortimer had now found.

She sent for the little maid's mother, and without finding fault with the child, said to her that she did not require her services any longer; and when the mother said, 'I hope it is for no fault that you part with her, ma'am?' she replied, evasively, 'Patience has her faults like other people;' and with that answer the mother was obliged to be satisfied.

When Patience was gone her mistress felt very unhappy. She had felt a pleasure in her company, because she was such a child, and so guileless. She had meant to keep her with her, and teach her so long as she lived, and trust her; but now all this was over, and she had nobody whom she chose to trust. The jackdaw, too, appeared to feel dull; there was nobody to play with him and carry him on her shoulder. He was dull, too, because he had lost that pretty necklace, for he often thought he should like to have it again to put among his treasures on the roof; therefore, he was fond of flying to the edge of the well, and gabbling there with great volubility; but I need not say that his chatter and his regret did not make the necklace float.

After a time, however, he found something else to amuse him, for one of Madam Mortimer's sons and his little boy came to visit her, and the jackdaw delighted in teasing the little fellow, and pecking his heels, and stealing his bits of string, and hiding his pencils; while the boy, on the other hand, was constantly teasing the bird, stroking his feathers the wrong way, snatching away his crusts, and otherwise plaguing him.

'I wish Patience was here to play with that child, and keep him from teasing my Jack,' said the old lady, fretfully. 'I get so infirm that children are a trouble to me.'

'Who is Patience?' asked her son.

So then Madam Mortimer told him the whole story; the boy and the jackdaw having previously gone out of the room together — the boy tantalizing him, and the bird gabbling and pecking at his ankles. When she had finished, her son said, 'Mother, I believe this will end in your suspecting me next! Why did you not ascertain whether the girl was innocent or guilty before you parted with her?'

'I feel certain she is guilty,' answered the mother, 'and I never mean to trust any servant again.'

'But if you could be certain she was innocent?' asked the son.

'Why, then I would never suspect a servant again, I think,' she replied. 'Certainly I should never suspect her — she seemed as open as the day — and you do not know, son, what a painful thing it is to have nobody about me that I can trust.'

'Excuse me, mother,' replied the son, 'you mean

nobody that you do trust; for all your servants have been with you for years, and deserve to be trusted, as far as we can see.'

'Well, well,' said the mother, 'it makes me unhappy enough, I assure you, to be obliged to suspect everybody; and if I could have that child back I should be truly glad; but I cannot harbor a thief.'

At this point of the discourse the boy and the jackdaw were heard in the yard making such a noise, and quarrelling, that the son went down, at his mother's request, to see what was the matter. 'He is a thief,' said the boy; 'I saw him fly to the roof with a long bit of blue ribbon that belongs to cook.'

The jackdaw gabbled angrily in reply, and it is highly probable that he understood part of the accusation, for he ruffled his feathers, and hopped about in a very excited way; and as the boy kept pointing at him, jeering him, the bird at last flew at him angrily, and gave him a very severe peck with a loud croak, that might have been meant to express, 'Take that.'

Having it on his hands to make up this quarrel, the little boy's father could not go on with the discourse he had begun with his mother at that time; but when he found another opportunity he said a great deal to her; and if it had not been that the jackdaw's suspicions being aroused, that troublesome bird would insist on listening to all he said, with his head on one side, and his twinkling eye fixed on his face, — and if he would have been quiet, instead of incessantly changing his place, as if he thought he could hear better on the right arm of the chair than the left, it is possible that the gentleman's discourse might have had a great effect on the old lady's mind; as it was, he interrupted his mistress's attention so much, that it is doubtful whether she remembered what her son had been talking of. And there was no sooner a pause in what the jackdaw probably regarded as a disagreeable subject, than he hopped to a private little cupboard that he kept under the turned-up edge of the carpet, and bringing out five or six mouldy bits of bread, laid them in a row on the rug before his mistress and her son, and walking about before them with an air of reflection, seemed as if he would have said, 'I must attend to my business, whether people talk or not.'

'I never saw such a queer fellow in my life as that bird is!' exclaimed the son.

'Why, Jack, you miser!' said his mistress; 'one would think you were starved.'

The jackdaw gabbled something which was no doubt meant for impertinence, till hearing footsteps outside the door, he hastily snatched up some of his mouldy property and flew with it to the top of the cabinet; then he stood staring at the remainder, fluttering his wings, and making a great outcry, for he did not dare to fly down for it, because his little tormentor had just rushed into the room.

'Papa, papa!' exclaimed the boy.

'Hold your tongue, Jack,' cried the grandmother; 'one at a time is enough.'

'Come, I will take you on my knee,' said his father, 'and then the daw will fly down for his bread.'

The daw no sooner saw his little enemy in a place of safety than he descended, snatched up his bread, and having secured it all, came again to give the boy a malicious little peck.

'Now what do you want to say?' asked his father.

'Papa,' repeated the boy, 'do currants ever grow under water?'

'No,' said his father.

'But,' replied the boy, 'there is something growing in the well, just under water, that looks like currants; and, papa, will you get it for me, please, for I should like to have it if it is good to eat.'

'Pooh!' said his grandmother; 'the boy is dreaming.'

But the boy made such a fuss about the bunch of currants, and was so positive as to their growing down in the well, that though it was now autumn, and the leaves were falling, and all the currants were either eaten up or stowed away in jam pots long before, his father and grandmother allowed him to take them to the well; but first the latter put on her black silk bonnet and her cloak, and fetched her stick from its place, lamenting all the while that Patience was not there to do all her little errands for her.

Now the weather all that summer and autumn had been remarkably dry, and the consequence was, that this old well, which had long been disused because it contained so little water, had now less than ever; but that little was clear; though when the old lady and her son looked over the edge they could not at first see down into it, because a few drops of rain had fallen, and had wetted the fern leaves which were still dripping a little and covering its surface with dimples.

'There are no red currants here, nor plums either, my child,' said the grandmother; and as she spoke she put down her gold-headed stick and shook the tuft of ferns that had been dripping, till she had shaken down all the water they contained.

The surface was now covered with little eddies and dimples. But when the water grew smooth again, 'There they are!' exclaimed the boy; 'there are the currants. Look, grandmother, they lie just under the shadow of those long leaves.'

'I see something,' replied his grandmother, shading her eyes; 'but it is six times as long as a bunch of currants, and the berries are three times as large. I shouldn't wonder, son, if that was my cornelian necklace.'

'I will see if we can ascertain,' said her son; 'there are several ladders about the premises, and the well is not at all deep.' So off he went, leaving the old lady and her grandson to look at the necklace; but the jackdaw, having by this time missed his mistress from her accustomed haunts, and being suspicious lest she might be inspecting some of his hoards, had set a search on foot for her, and now flew up screaming and making a great outcry, as if he thought he was going to be robbed. However, having lighted on the edge of the well, and observed that the necklace was there all safe, he felt more at his ease; and, if his mistress could have understood the tongue of a daw, she would have now heard him relate how he threw it there; as it was, she only heard him gabble, and saw him now and then peck at the boy's pinafore. When the jackdaw saw a ladder brought, however, his mind misgave him that his mistress meant to get the necklace out again; and his thievish spirit sank very low. However, being a politic bird, he was quite silent while the ladder was lowered, and while the gardener's boy descended to the bottom of the well and groped about with his hands, for there was not a foot of water. 'There is my necklace, sure enough,' exclaimed the old lady as the boy lifted up the long row of shining beads; 'bring it out, James.' 'Please, ma'am, here's the great silver skewer that was lost a year ago,' exclaimed the boy; 'and, dear me, here's the nozzle of a candlestick.'

The old lady held up her hands; she had parted with a good cook, in consequence of the loss of this skewer. But the sight of the necklace dangling from the youth's hand as he prepared to mount the ladder was too much for the jackdaw.—he suddenly flew down, gave the hand a tremendous peck with his hard bill, and while the boy cried out and dropped the necklace, the bird made a sudden dart at it, snatched it before it touched the water, and flew up with it into a tree. There he rested a few minutes playing with the wet necklace, and shaking it in the sunlight; but not all his mistress's entreaties and coaxing could bring him down, and in a few minutes he flew off again and settled on the roof of the house.

There, in less than ten minutes, he was found by his mistress and her son, with all his ill-gotten gains spread out before him; everything was taken from him, and when his mistress saw the articles whose loss had caused her to suspect almost every one about her of theft, she was so vexed that she actually shed tears. 'Mother,' said her son, 'it appears to me that you have trusted the only creature about you that was utterly unworthy of trust!'

The old lady was so much disheartened that she could not say a word; but such is the audacity of a jackdaw's nature, that not half an hour after this, when the foot-boy brought in the tea things, Jack walked in after him with a grave expression of countenance and hopped on to the tea table as if nothing had happened.

'Patience shall come back again,' thought the old lady; 'I'll send for her and her mother, and I'll never suspect her any more. It is plain enough now that Jack must have thrown my property down there.'

So the mother of Patience was sent for; but, alas, what disappointments people are doomed to! The mother expressed herself much obliged to Madam Mortimer, but said, that her cousin, in London, hearing that she was out of place, had sent for her to serve in her shop. 'And that I look on as a great rise in life for her,' said the mother, with an air of satisfaction: 'and I am going to send a box of clothes to her next week,' she continued, 'and I shall tell her, ma'am, that you have not forgotten her.'

Madam Mortimer was very much vexed; but the necklace was in her hand, and a sudden thought struck her that she would give it to Patience. So she said, with a sigh, 'Well, Mrs. Grey, when you send the box, you may put this in it.'

Her mother at first looked pleased, but she presently drew back, and said, 'Thank you, kindly, ma'am, but that necklace is by far too fine for my Patience, and it might do her harm to have it, and I never encourage her to wish for fine clothes.'

'Good evening, then,' said Madam Mortimer; and as the woman went away, she walked softly to the hole in the blind, and watched her talking and laughing with the cook, rather, as it seemed, in a triumphant way, as if she was exulting in the good fortune of her child, and the evident discomfiture of her former mistress. 'It is entirely the fault of that thieving jackdaw,' said the old lady, as she returned to her chair; and as she spoke she saw the suspicious bird, sitting listening to her with his head on one side. 'It is enough to make anybody suspicious to lose things as I have lost them,' she thought. 'However, I shall soon leave off the habit, as I find it a bad one. I wonder whether that woman is gone yet; I'll just take a peep, and see what they are about, gossiping, down there. Ah, there she is! I wish I hadn't sent Patience away; but, perhaps, if I had been kinder to her than I was, she would have given me cause to suspect her before long.'

Madam Mortimer then settled herself in her chair and began to doze. When she awoke, the necklace was gone again; and perhaps it is a proof that she really was somewhat improved, that though she said, 'I suspect, Jack, you know where that necklace is,' she never took any steps in the matter, but left her glittering stones in the bird's greedy keeping; and after taking a little time for consideration, put a patch upon the hole in the blind, so that she could never look through it any more. Whether she was cured of her suspicious turn of mind is more than I can tell, but it is certain that she henceforth looked on suspicions as undesirable, and seldom thought of little Patience without a sigh.

THE MINNOWS WITH SILVER TAILS.

THE MINNOWS WITH SILVER TAILS.

THERE was a cuckoo-clock hanging in Tom Turner's cottage. When it struck One, Tom's wife laid the baby in the cradle, and took a saucepan off the fire, from which came a very savory smell.

Her two little children, who had been playing in the open doorway, ran to the table, and began softly to drum upon it with their pewter spoons, looking eagerly at their mother as she turned a nice little piece of pork into a dish, and set greens and potatoes round it. They fetched the salt; then they set a chair for their father; brought their own stools; and pulled their mother's rocking-chair close to the table.

'Run to the door, Billy,' said the mother, 'and see if father's coming.' Billy ran to the door; and, after the fashion of little children, looked first the right way, and then the wrong way, but no father was to be seen.

Presently the mother followed him, and shaded her eyes with her hand, for the sun was hot. 'If father doesn't come soon,' she observed, 'the apple-dumpling will be too much done, by a deal.'

'There he is!' cried the little boy, 'he is coming

round by the wood; and now he's going over the bridge. O father! make haste, and have some apple-dumpling.'

'Tom,' said his wife, as he came near, 'art tired to-day?'

'Uncommon tired,' said Tom, and he threw himself on the bench, in the shadow of the thatch.

'Has anything gone wrong?' asked his wife; 'what's the matter?'

'Matter?' repeated Tom, 'is anything the matter? The matter is this, mother, that I'm a miserable hard-worked slave;' and he clapped his hands upon his knees, and muttered in a deep voice, which frightened the children — 'a miserable slave!'

'Bless us!' said the wife, and could not make out what he meant.

'A miserable ill-used slave,' continued Tom, 'and always have been.'

'Always have been?' said his wife; 'why, father, I thought thou used to say, at the election time, that thou wast a free-born Briton?'

'Women have no business with politics,' said Tom, getting up rather sulkily. And whether it was the force of habit, or the smell of the dinner, that made him do it, has not been ascertained; but it is certain that he walked into the house, ate plenty of pork and greens, and then took a tolerable share in demolishing the apple-dumpling.

When the little children were gone out to play, his wife said to him, 'Tom, I hope thou and master haven't had words to-day?'

'*Master*,' said Tom, 'yes, a pretty master he has

been; and a pretty slave I've been. Don't talk to me of masters.'

'O Tom, Tom,' cried his wife, 'but he's been a good master to you; fourteen shillings a week, regular wages, — that's not a thing to make a sneer at; and think how warm the children are lapped up o' winter nights, and you with as good shoes to your feet as ever keep him out of the mud.'

'What of that?' said Tom; 'isn't my labor worth the money? I'm not beholden to my employer. He gets as good from me as he gives.'

'Very like, Tom. There's not a man for miles round that can match you at a graft; and as to early peas — but if master can't do without you, I'm sure you can't do without him. O, dear, to think that you and he should have had words!'

'We've had no words,' said Tom, impatiently; 'but I'm sick of being at another man's beck and call. It's "Tom do this," and "Tom do that," and nothing but work, work, work, from Monday morning till Saturday night; and I was thinking, as I walked over to Squire Morton's to ask for the turnip seed for master — I was thinking, Sally, that I am nothing but a poor working man after all. In short, I'm a *slave*, and my spirit won't stand it.'

So saying, Tom flung himself out at the cottage door, and his wife thought he was going back to his work as usual. But she was mistaken; he walked to the wood, and there, when he came to the border of a little tinkling stream, he sat down, and began to brood over his grievances. It was a very hot day.

'Now, I'll tell you what,' said Tom to himself, 'it's

a great deal pleasanter sitting here in the shade than broiling over celery trenches; and then thinning of wall fruit, with a baking sun at one's back, and a hot wall before one's eyes. But I'm a miserable slave. I must either work or see 'em starve; a very hard lot it is to be a workingman. But it is not only the work that I complain of, but being obliged to work just as *he* pleases. It's enough to spoil any man's temper to be told to dig up those asparagus beds just when they were getting to be the very pride of the parish. And what for? Why, to make room for Madam's new gravel walk, that she mayn't wet her feet going over the grass. Now, I ask you,' continued Tom, still talk- to himself, 'whether that isn't enough to spoil any man's temper?'

'Ahem!' said a voice close to him.

Tom started, and to his great surprise, saw a small man, about the size of his own baby sitting composedly at his elbow. He was dressed in green — green hat, green coat, and green shoes. He had very bright black eyes, and they twinkled very much as he looked at Tom and smiled.

'Servant, sir!' said Tom, edging himself a little farther off.

'Miserable slave,' said the small man, ' art thou so far lost to the noble sense of freedom that thy very salutation acknowledges a mere stranger as thy master!'

'Who are you,' said Tom, 'and how dare you call me a slave?'

'Tom,' said the small man, with a knowing look, 'don't speak roughly. Keep your rough words for your wife, my man; she is bound to bear them — what else is she for, in fact?'

'I'll thank you to let my affairs alone,' interrupted Tom, shortly.

'Tom, I'm your friend; I think I can help you out of your difficulty. I admire your spirit. Would *I* demean myself to work for a master, and attend to all his whims?' As he said this the small man stooped and looked very earnestly into the stream. Drip, drip, drip, went the water over a little fall in the stones, and wetted the watercresses till they shone in the light, while the leaves fluttered overhead and checkered the moss with glittering spots of sunshine. Tom watched the small man with earnest attention as he turned over the leaves of the cresses. At last he saw him snatch something, which looked like a little fish, out of the water, and put it in his pocket.

'It's my belief, Tom,' he said, resuming the conversation, 'that you have been puzzling your head with what people call Political Economy.'

'Never heard of such a thing,' said Tom. 'But I've been thinking that I don't see why I'm to work any more than those that employ me.'

'Why, you see, Tom, you must have money. Now it seems to me that there are but four ways of getting money: there's Stealing' —

'Which won't suit *me*,' interrupted Tom.

'Very good. Then there's Borrowing' —

'Which I don't want to do.'

'And there's Begging' —

'No, thank you,' said Tom, stoutly.

'And there's giving money's worth for the money; that is to say, Work, Labor.'

'Your words are as fine as a sermon,' said Tom.

'But look here, Tom,' proceeded the man in green, drawing his hand out of his pocket, and showing a little dripping fish in his palm, 'what do you call this?'

'I call it a very small minnow,' said Tom.

'And do you see anything particular about its tail?'

'It looks uncommon bright,' answered Tom, stooping to look at it.

'It does,' said the man in green, 'and now I'll tell you a secret, for I'm resolved to be your friend. Every minnow in this stream — they are very scarce, mind you — but every one of them has a silver tail.'

'You don't say so,' exclaimed Tom, opening his eyes very wide; 'fishing for minnows, and being one's own master, would be a great deal pleasanter than the sort of life I've been leading this many a day.'

'Well, keep the secret as to where you get them; and much good may it do you,' said the man in green. 'Farewell, I wish you joy of your freedom.' So saying, he walked away, leaving Tom on the brink of the stream, full of joy and pride.

He went to his master, and told him that he had an opportunity for *bettering* himself, and should not work for him any longer. The next day he arose with the dawn, and went to work to search for minnows. But of all the minnows in the world never were any so nimble as those with silver tails. They were very shy, too, and had as many turns and doubles as a hare; what a life they led him! They made him troll up the stream for miles; then, just as he thought his chase was at an end, and he was sure of them, they would leap quite out of the water, and dart down the stream again like little silver arrows. Miles and miles he went, tired, and wet, and hungry. He came home late in the evening, completely wearied and footsore, with only three minnows in his pocket, each with a silver tail.

'But at any rate,' he said to himself, as he lay down in his bed, 'though they lead me a pretty life, and I have to work harder than ever, yet I certainly am free; no man can order me about now.'

This went on for a whole week; he worked very hard; but on Saturday afternoon he had only caught fourteen minnows.

'If it wasn't for the pride of the thing,' he said to himself, 'I'd have no more to do with fishing for minnows. This is the hardest work I ever did. I am quite a slave to them. I rush up and down, I dodge in and out, I splash myself, and fret myself, and broil myself in the sun, and all for the sake of a dumb thing, that gets the better of me with a wag of its fins. But it's no use standing here talking; I must set off to the town and sell them, or Sally will wonder why I don't bring her the week's money.' So he walked to the town, and offered his fish for sale as great curiosities.

'Very pretty,' said the first people he showed them to; but 'they never bought anything that was not useful.'

'Were they good to eat?' asked the woman at the

next house. 'No! Then they would not have them.'

'Much too dear,' said a third.

'And not so very curious,' said a fourth; 'but they hoped he had come by them honestly.'

At the fifth house they said, 'O! pooh!' when he exhibited them. 'No, no, they were not quite so silly as to believe there were fish in the world with silver tails; if there had been, they should often have heard of them before.'

At the sixth house they were such a very long time turning over his fish, pinching their tails, bargaining, and discussing them, that he ventured to remonstrate, and request that they would make more haste. Thereupon they said if he did not choose to wait their pleasure, they would not purchase at all. So they shut the door upon him; and as this soured his temper, he spoke rather roughly at the next two houses, and was dismissed at once as a very rude, uncivil person.

But after all, his fish were really great curiosities; and when he had exhibited them all over the town, set them out in all lights, praised their perfections, and taken immense pains to conceal his impatience and ill-temper, he at length contrived to sell them all, and got exactly fourteen shillings for them, and no more.

'Now, I'll tell you what, Tom Turner,' he said to himself, 'in my opinion you've been making a great fool of yourself, and I only hope Sally will not find it out. You was tired of being a workingman, and that man in green has cheated you into doing the hardest week's work you ever did in your life, by making you believe it was more free-like and easier. Well, you said you didn't mind it, because you had no master; but I've found out this afternoon, Tom, and I don't mind your knowing it, that every one of those customers of yours was your master just the same. Why! you were at the beck of every man, woman, and child that came near you — obliged to be in a good temper, too, which was very aggravating.'

'True, Tom,' said the man in green, starting up in his path, 'I knew you were a man of sense; look you, you're *all* workingmen, and you must all please your customers. Your master was your customer; what he bought of you was your work. Well, you must let the work be such as will please the customer.'

'*All* workingmen; how do you make that out?' said Tom, chinking the fourteen shillings in his hand. 'Is my master a workingman; and has he got a master of his own? Nonsense!'

'No nonsense at all; — he works with his head, keeps his books, and manages his great works. He has many masters, else why was he nearly ruined last year?'

'He was nearly ruined because he made some new-fangled kind of patterns at his works, and people would not buy them,' said Tom. 'Well, in a way of speaking, then, he works to please his masters, poor fellow! He is, as one may say, a fellow-servant, and plagued with very awkward masters! So I should not mind his being my master, and I think I'll go and tell him so.'

'I would, Tom,' said the man in green. 'Tell him you have not been able to *better* yourself, and you have no objection now to dig up the asparagus bed.'

So Tom trudged home to his wife, gave her the money he had earned, got his old master to take him back, and kept a profound secret his adventures with the man in green, and the fish with the silver tails.

I HAVE A RIGHT.

WE, as a nation, are remarkably fond of talking about our rights. The expression, 'I have a right,' is constantly in our mouths. This is one reason, among some others, why it is fortunate for us that we speak English, since this favorite phrase in more than one continental tongue has no precise equivalent.

Whether the nation's phrase grew out of the nation's character, or whether the happy possession of such a phrase has helped to mould that character, it is scarcely now worth while to inquire. Certain it is that those generations which make proverbs, make thereby laws which govern their children's children, and thus, perhaps, it comes to pass that this neat, independent, Anglo-Saxon phrase helps to get and keep for us the very rights it tells of. For, as under some governments it is true that the dearest and most inalienable *rights* of the race go by the name of privilege, indulgence, or immunity, a concession, and not an inheritance; a gift, and not a birthright; while ancient rights, in our sense of this word, merge into mere privileges held at the ruler's will, and having been once called privileges, may be exchanged by him for other privileges which may amount to no more than the sight of a glittering show; so in our case it is true that privileges have a constant tendency to merge into rights. Let any man grant his neighbors the privilege of walking through his fields, his park, or his grounds, and then see how soon it will be said that they have a right to traverse them; and in fact very soon they *will* have a right by the law of the land; for, to prove the right, they need only show that they have enjoyed the privilege 'time out of mind.' And then, again, *Right* is very unfair to his cousin *Privilege*, for, by the laws of England, sixty years constitute 'time out of mind.'

By taking the trouble to investigate, any person may find many parallel cases, and so we keep the path of liberty. First we got that path as a sort of privilege which was winked at; then we made out that we had a right to it! next we proved that it wanted widening, and then we paved it handsomely, made a king's highway of it, and took pains to have it constantly in repair.

Now, it being an acknowledged thing, my dear friends, that we have rights, and that we like to have these facts well known to all whom it may concern — how glad you will be if I can point out to you certain rights which some of you have scarcely considered at all. I have met with numbers of worshipful old gentlemen, industrious young workmen, and women of all degrees, who knew well how to use our favorite phrase in its common vulgar sense; but I knew a worshipful old baker, in an old country town, who used it oftener than any of them. To hear him hold forth about his rights, did one's heart good, and made one proud of one's country. Everybody else's rights appeared flat and tame compared with his, and the best of it was, that no one was ever heard to dispute them.

Dear old man, he is dead now, but some of his rights survive him. I was on my way home to the neighborhood of that little country town wherein, for so many years, he might have been seen on a summer evening, standing in his shop door, and exercising the rights he loved, when it so happened that I heard some of my countrymen also discoursing about *their* rights, and the more they talked, the more petty and insignificant seemed their rights compared with those of Mr. Bryce, the baker.

We took our tickets at the London terminus of the Great Northern Railway, and entered an empty carriage; in a corner seat, however, a gentleman's greatcoat was lying; presently a lady got in, and now the two vacant seats were, it so happened, as far as possible, asunder.

The next arrivals were another lady with a little girl about four years old. Without any hesitation she took up the coat, and placing it in another corner seat, set her child in the division near herself.

Had she a right to do this? you inquire. Certainly not; and she was soon reminded of that fact, for just at the last minute a calm and rather supercilious looking young man entered, glanced coldly at her, and said, 'I must trouble you, madam, for that seat; I laid my coat on it some time ago, and also turned the cushion; I really *must* request you to leave it, as I have a right to it.'

He laid as strong an emphasis on the *must*, as if to turn her out was a stringent duty. Perhaps she thought so, for as she glanced, in rising, at the child, she said, with a smile at the youth, who was quite young enough to be her son, 'Certainly you have an undoubted right to this seat;' and then added, 'but I suppose no one would have disputed your right to give it up to me, if you had chosen.'

Her easy self-possession, and perhaps her remark, made him look a little awkward; but as the lady rose, my brother changed places with the child, and thus they still sat together; and while the youth settled himself in the place he had a right to, our train set off with one of those thrice horrible, wavering, and querulous screeches of which the Great Northern has a monopoly.

While we went through the first tunnel, rending the air all the time with terrific shrieks, the little girl held tightly by her mother's hand, and two large tears rolled down her rosy face. 'We shall soon be at Hornsey,' said her mother, and accordingly in a few minutes we stopped, and while the lady and child disappeared from our view, the owner of the seat ejaculated, 'Cool!' and then looking round the carriage, he continued, as appealing to those who were sure to agree with him—'When a man has a right to a thing, why, he *has* a right; but to have a right to waive a right, is a dodge that a man wouldn't expect to be told of.'

This most lucid speech he closed with a general smile, and we set off again with another shriek, longer and shriller than the former one.

I HAVE A RIGHT.

After an hour's travelling we were deserted by all our fellow-passengers, and seemed to be waiting a very long time at a little country station. At length two old gentlemen entered, and, as the railway man opened the door for them, I said to him, 'Can you tell me why we are detained here so long?'

'Yes, ma'am,' he replied; 'there's an excursion train due directly, and we're shunted off the line to let it pass.'

'Horrid bore!' said one old gentleman.

'Disgraceful shame!' said the other; 'but don't let that make you uneasy, young lady,' he added, politely addressing me; '"shunted" means nothing dangerous.'

I was about to ask what it did mean, when with a whiz, and a great noise of cheering, the excursion train shot past us, displaying a long, long succession of second and third-class carriages, every window garnished with pale faces of men and women, besides numbers of delicate-looking children.

'Disgraceful shame!' repeated the stoutest of the old gentlemen; 'here's our train twenty minutes late; twenty minutes, sir, by the clock.'

'I should think,' said my brother, 'that this is not a grievance of very frequent occurrence — mail trains are not often obliged to give way to the convenience of the excursionists; but we were behind time when we got up to this station, and as we must stop a quarter of an hour shortly, we should very much have detained that train if it had been on the same line, and behind us.'

'Well, I can't make it out,' was the reply; 'and

what does their being detained matter to me; I paid for my ticket and I've a right to be taken on.'

'Certainly,' said the other; 'no man has a right to interfere with my business for the sake of his pleasure — such new-fangled notions! — What's the good of a day's pleasure to the working classes?'

'They have it so seldom,' my brother suggested, 'that they have plenty of time to consider that question between one day's pleasure and the next.'

'Horrid bore, these excursion trains!' repeated the first speaker; 'filling the country with holiday folk; what do they want with holidays — much better stop at home, and work, and earn a little more. What's the good of sending out a swarm of pale-faced, knock-knee'd London artisans, and gaping children, that don't know a kite from a jackdaw? If you must give 'em a treat, let it be a good dinner. Country air, indeed! *I* don't find London unhealthy; and I spend three or four months in it every year.'

'To be sure,' echoed his companion, 'these London clergy and ministers ought to know better than to spread such sentimental nonsense among the people — duty comes before pleasure, doesn't it? Why, a man had the assurance to write to me — a perfect stranger — to know whether I'd open my park for a shoal of his cockney parishioners to dine and drink tea in! He knew it was closed, forsooth, but he hoped for once, and in the cause of philanthropy, I'd open it. I should like to know where my young coveys would be when every inch in my wood had been overrun, and all the bracken trod down in the cause of philanthropy? No, I wrote him a piece of my mind — I said, "Rev. Sir, I do not fence and guard my grounds that paupers may make a playground of them; and, though your request makes me question your good taste a little, I trust to your good sense not to render your people liable to be taken up as trespassers. I have a right to prosecute all trespassers in my grounds, and, therefore, I advise you to keep your people clear of them."'

'And very proper, too,' replied the other; 'there are plenty of people that will receive them; there's your neighbor, Sir Edward, who's happy and proud to entertain as many as they like to pour into his domain.'

Upon this they both laughed, as it appeared, in pity of the said Sir Edward. 'Well, well, every man has a right to his own opinion.' (N. B., is that a fact?) 'Sir Edward wanted me, the other day, to subscribe to some new baths and wash-houses. "My good fellow," I said, "when all the paupers in London can earn their own living, it will be time enough to talk of washing their faces; but for goodness' sake let 'em earn dinners before you offer 'em Windsor soap, and hats before you find 'em pomatum."'

'And may I know what Sir Edward said in reply?' I inquired, addressing the old gentleman.

He seemed to consider. 'Well,' he said, after a puzzled pause, 'it was something of this sort — something about the decencies of life being striven for with better heart, if a few of its amenities were within reach.'

This reminded me of a poor woman who lived in a particularly dirty cottage, near my father's house, in the country. I one day tapped at her door, and she opened it in a gown all spotted with white-wash. 'What! cleaning, Mrs. Matts?' I exclaimed in surprise. 'Why, yes, Miss,' she replied, 'for my husband's brother has just been up from London, where he works, to see us, and brought us a beautiful *pictur* of the Queen, all in a gilt frame, Miss; and when he'd hung it up, it made the walls look so shocking dirty, that I couldn't abear the sight of 'em, so I'm cleaning, you see.'

But enough has been said about the rights of other people; let us now turn to Mr. Bryce, the baker.

Bryce was working for a baker in the village near which my grandfather lived. His master died suddenly, leaving a widow and nine children. Bryce was an enterprising young man, and had been thinking of setting up for himself. My grandfather, however, heard that after his master's death he gave up this wish, and continued to work at his former wages, trying to keep the business together for the widow. Happening to meet him, he asked him if this report were true?

'Why, yes, sir,' said Bryce; 'you see nobody else would manage everything for her without a share of the profits; and nine children — what a tug they are! so as I have nobody belonging to me — nobody that has any claim on me —'

'But I thought you wanted to set up for yourself?'

'And so I did, sir; and if I'd a wife and family, I'd make a push to get on for their sakes, — but I've none; and so, as I can live on what I get, and hurt nobody by it, "*I have a right*" to help her, poor soul, as I've a mind to.'

Soon after this the widow took to dress-making, and did so well that she wanted no help from Bryce, who now set up for himself, and borrowed a sum of money from my grandfather to begin with. At first he was so poor, and the weekly profits were so small, that he requested my grandfather to receive the trifle of interest monthly, and for the first two months he said it 'completely cleared him out' to pay it. My grandfather was, therefore, rather surprised one Saturday evening, as he sauntered down the village street, to see four decrepit old people hobbling down the steps of his shop, each carrying a good-sized loaf, and loudly praising the generosity of Mr. Bryce. The sun was just setting, and cast a ruddy glow on the young baker's face as he stood leaning against the post of his door, but he started with some confusion when he saw my grandfather, and hastily asked him to enter his shop. 'I reckon you are surprised, sir,' he said, 'to see me giving away bread before I've paid my debt: but just look round, sir. Those four loaves were all I had left, except what I can eat myself, and they were stale; so think what they'd have been by Monday morning.'

'I don't wish to interfere with your charities,' said my grandfather.

'But, sir,' said Bryce, 'I want you to see that I'm as eager to pay off that money as I can be; but people won't buy stale bread—they won't, indeed; and so I thought *I had a right* to give away those four loaves, being they were left upon my hands.'

'I think so too,' said my grandfather, who was then quite a young man, 'and I shall think so next Saturday and the Saturday after.'

'Thank you, sir, I'm sure,' said the baker.

In course of time the debt was paid, though almost every Saturday those old people hobbled from the door. And now Mr. Bryce's rights were found to increase with his business and enlarge with his family.

First he had only *a right* to give away the stale loaves, 'being he was in debt.' Then *he had a right* to give away all that was left, 'being he was out of debt.' While he was single, *he had a right* to bake dinners for nothing, 'being he had no family to save for.' When he was married, *he had a right* to consider the poor, 'being, as he was, so prosperous as to have enough for his own, and something over.' When he had ten children, business still increasing, he found out that *he had a right* to adopt his wife's little niece, 'for, bless you, sir,' he observed, 'I've such a lot of my own, that a pudding that serves for ten shares serves for eleven just as well. And, as for schooling, I wouldn't think of it, if my boys and girls were not as good scholars as I'd wish to see; for I spare nothing for their learning — but being they are, and money still in the till, *why, I've a right* to let this little one share. In fact, when a man has earned a jolly hot dinner for his family every day, and seen 'em say their grace over it, *he has a right* to give what they leave on't to the needy, especially if his wife's agreeable.'

And so Mr. Bryce, the baker, went on prospering, and finding out new rights to keep pace with his prosperity. In due time his many sons and daughters grew up; the latter married, and the former were placed out in life. Finally, after a long and happy life, Mr. Bryce, the baker, died, and in his will, after leaving £500 apiece to all his sons and daughters, he concluded his bequests with this characteristic sentence:—

'And, my dear children, by the blessing of God, having put you out well in life, and left you all handsome, I feel (especially as I have the hearty consent of you all) that I have a right to leave the rest of my property, namely £700, for the use of those that want it. First, the village of D—— being very much in want of good water, I leave £400, the estimated cost, for digging a well, and making a pump over it, the same to be free to all; and the interest of the remainder I leave to be spent in blankets every winter, and given away to the most destitute widows and orphans in the parish.'

So the well was dug, and the pump was made; and as long as the village lasts, opposite his own shop door, the sparkling water will gush out; the village mothers will gossip as they fill their buckets there; the village fathers will cool their sunburnt foreheads there, and the village children will put their ears to it and listen to its purling down below; a witness to the rights, and a proof of how his rights were used by Bryce the baker.

THE MOORISH GOLD.

A LONG while ago, says the legend, when the dominion of the Moors was beginning to decline in Spain, it was rumored on a certain day, in Toledo, that the Christians were coming down in great force to besiege the city, and had vowed that they would desecrate the Mosque, and despoil it of its gold and jewels — that they would fight their way over the bridge of the Tagus, and bear away the choicest of its treasures from the great Alcazar of Toledo.

But a few days before these tidings arrived, a marvellous stupor had come upon the Moorish masters of the city; some said it was the heat, but they had never cared for the heat before, since they came from a hotter region. They walked about, it is true, but it was slowly, and in the great shadows of their houses, and if any man crossed over the street, he held his hand to his forehead and sighed. A few were so faint that they lay down to rest on the steps of the Alcazar; they thought the scent of the pomegranate flowers oppressed them, though none had complained of this scent before. Others believed that it was a thin vapor which rose up in the heat from the glassy bosom of the Tagus, and spread out like steam above the highest roofs, making the sun look red and fiery.

In spite of this, says the legend, they set about defending themselves; and the danger being imminent, they shipped great store of costly merchandise, with jewels, and gold, and coined money, on board their vessels, which lay in the Tagus, and sent them off, to the number of five, with orders to drop down the river, double the Cape St. Vincent, and sail up the Guadalquivir, that their precious lading might be given over into the keeping of the Moorish King of Seville.

But alas, says the legend, of those five fair vessels, not one ever cast anchor before the walls of Seville, for a great wind took them, scattered and drove them northward as soon as they were clear of the Tagus, and it is supposed that four of the five foundered with their crews and their lading, for they never were heard of more.

It was supposed so, says the legend, but the Moorish masters of Toledo had little time to fret themselves for their sunken treasure, since that same week the plague appeared, and while the Christians were harassing them without, they lay in the still heat and perished in the streets by hundreds and by thousands within.

One vessel was left, and day after day, in the wind and the storm, she drove still farther northward, and that strange lethargy had crept on board with the sailors, though now there was neither any heat, nor scent of pomegranate flowers, to plead as a reason for it. And now the white cliffs of a great island were visible, and they said to themselves that they should never behold the sunny country of Spain any more, but be cast ashore at the end of the earth, in the kingdom of William the Norman.

Still the north wind raged, and the foaming billows broke — that was a long and fearful gale: some of the sailors died at the oar, but it was neither hunger nor toil that killed them; and when at last the wind dropped suddenly, and the vessel drifted on to a sandy shore, only three men sprang out from her. There were but three survivors, for the plague had come on board with them and their treasure.

These three men sprang ashore; they landed one coffer filled with gold, precious stones, and coined money. It was as much as their failing strength could do. The islanders fell back from them, for they had seen the dark faces of the dead Moors as they lay in the plague-stricken vessel. They did not molest the sailors, but let them sit alone on the shore bemoaning their fate till night came on, and their vessel at high tide drifted out again to sea, while these three desolate men took up the coffer and went inland, up and up, among the Cumberland hills.

It was as much as they could carry, but no man cared to help. They wandered about among the mountains, and the last time they were seen, it was apparent that they had hidden their treasure in some cavern, or sunk it in the earth, or heaved a stone upon it; for the coffer was gone. Soon after, the men disappeared also; but whether they perished among the rocks, or died of the plague, none could tell; but though many and many a cavern has been searched, and many a stone displaced, from that day to this, says the legend, no man has ever set eyes upon the glittering Moorish gold.

So much for legend; now for more authentic narrative.

An old gentleman sat in a boat on one of the loveliest of the English lakes, and looked up at the mountains with delight.

'Glorious!' he exclaimed; 'superb! it beats Switzerland out and out.'

Whether he was right is nothing to the purpose, but he said it. He was stout, had a red face, blue spectacles, and a straw hat tied to his button-hole with black ribbon.

Now, when he exclaimed, 'It beats Switzerland out and out!' his footman sitting opposite to him, and thinking the observation called for an answer, replied, with prompt respect, 'Certainly, sir, no doubt.'

Thereupon his master looked at his fat white face, which expressed no manner of enthusiasm, but rather showed an absorbing interest in the provision basket which he held on his knee.

'Pray, Richard,' said the old gentleman, 'do you take any pleasure in the beauties of Nature?'

Richard pondered, and answered as before, respectfully, 'Not in particular, sir.'

'It's for want of knowing more about them,' said his master, good-humoredly; 'to-morrow I am going up a mountain to see such a view as everybody must delight in — you shall go too.'

Richard touched his hat.

The next morning the old gentleman, with two others, quite as enthusiastic, but by no means so fat, and with a guide, and two hampers containing patties, pigeon-pies, hard-boiled eggs, potted salmon, new bread and butter, and water-cresses, set off, his servant accompanying .him, to see the beauties of Nature among the mountains.

How many times the gentlemen exclaimed, 'Glorious! hot day! fine view! lovely scenery!' it is impossible to say. How many times the footman wished himself at home, cleaning his plate, waiting at table, or doing anything in the world but climbing a mountain, it is also impossible to say. Happily for him the path got so steep, and the day got so hot, that all at once the gentlemen bethought themselves of luncheon, and decided that the very spot where they then stood was the right one to take it in.

So the guide, not by any means disinclined to rest, led them a little aside, and turning the angle of a steep rock, suddenly introduced them to a little quiet nook enclosed with high rocks. It was about the size, Richard thought, of the back parlor at home, only it was open to the sky, and its walls were hung with foxgloves, broom, tufts of heath in blossom, and a few trailing eglantines, instead of pictures and looking-glasses. How still the place was, and how blue the sky above!

'Well, Richard,' said his master, 'what did you think of the view?'

Richard replied as before, respectfully, 'That he had been wondering at it all the way up; everything below looked so small, in particular the hay-stacks; the round ones, he observed, had reminded him of queen-cakes, and the square ones of penny sponge-cakes or quartern loaves, just exactly that shape, and certainly no bigger.'

His master was disappointed to find that Richard's comparison was queer enough to make both the other gentlemen laugh — not, however, at the footman, but at his master, for expecting him to relish the scenery.

They soon rose from their lunch. It was a sin, they said, to waste the sweet weather in that nook; they should go higher; but Richard might stay behind, if he liked, and pack the baskets; if he had not had enough to eat either, his master said he was to help himself.

'Thank you, sir, I'm sure,' said Richard, gratefully.

Accordingly, when they were gone, he *did* pack the baskets, regaling himself with many a tit-bit meanwhile. This pleasing duty fulfilled, he stretched himself under the steep sandstone walls of his roofless room, basked in the hot sun, looked up into the glowing sky, whistled, and fanned himself with some twigs of broom, which were covered thick with flowers like yellow butterflies.

A thicket of broom bushes grew against the side of the rock, and as he stretched out his hand to one of them to pull off another bough, the bush swung back to its place, and a bird flew out so close to him that she swept his forehead with her wings.

He peeped into the bush. Yes, it was, as he had thought, a nest — as pretty as moss and feathers could make it; and with four pink eggs in it, quite warm and half transparent; he parted the thick branches of the broom, and as he held them so, a sunbeam struck between them, and showed a little hole in the rock close to the ground; it looked, he thought, much as the arch of a bridge might look, if the river beneath was so high as to reach within a few inches of the key-stone. He pushed himself further into the broom, and with his hands idly swept down the soft sand, and let it slide down a little rise till it had buried to their heads some tall bluebells that grew there. Then he noticed that the arch, as more of it became disclosed, was very regular for a natural opening, and as the sand slipped away, it revealed the top of what seemed a worm-eaten wooden door, which fitted it with tolerable accuracy. Nearly a foot of this door was visible, when Richard, impatient to know what was behind it, took a stone, and striking the old wood with some force, drove in a small portion of it. He withdrew his head that the light might shine into it; there was a deep cavity, and a narrow sunbeam entering, glittered and trembled upon something which lay on the sand in a heap within, and was red and fiery.

His heart beat quick, his eyes became accustomed to the dim light within, he could see bags lying side by side; one of them had burst open, its contents were large coins — surely gold coins — the sunbeam was red upon their rims; yes, they were gold, they were unknown, they were unclaimed, they were his!

He withdrew his eyes. The broom boughs swung back again and concealed the opening; he sat down, propped his head upon his hands, and a whirling, wondering sense of possession, together with a suffocating fear that he should never be able to grasp all his treasure unshared, strove within him, and threw him into such a fever of excitement, that for a while he could scarcely move or breathe. At last he mastered these feelings, forced himself again into the thicket, and thought he should never be satisfied with staring in again and again at the glittering, gleaming gold.

Incalculable riches, and all to be his own!

Yes, *all;* he had heard of such people as Lords of the Manor, his master was one down in the south, but Richard did not mean to consider the law; they should all be his own. He would secure them, buy a fine house, and eat, drink, and dress of the very best. He exulted, as in that quiet nook alone he capered and laughed aloud; then he sat down and began to arrange his thoughts.

Let us see, should he open his heart and share them with his brother? Share them! nonsense; no. What had his brother done for him? Why, only this — when Richard was out of place this brother gave him two sovereigns out of his own wages, and afterwards he spared with difficulty five shillings more. Now his brother never expected to see it again. Well, Richard decided to exceed his expectations; he would return it, every farthing: possibly he might give him another sovereign besides. Then there were his two sisters. As to the elder, she certainly had been very good to him; she had many children, and worked hard, yet when Richard was taken ill she had nursed him, and sheltered him, and sat up with him at night; she had been a true and tried friend to him. Well, he would reward her; he would send her all his clothes; for of course he should in future dress like a gentleman. He would also send her five pounds. No; what would be the use of that? Her drunken husband would only squander it all away; perhaps, instead of that, he would adopt one of her boys— that would be so good, so generous, it would surely be full payment. Or, perhaps it would be better to pay his schooling, and let him live at home; if he were brought into a fine house he might grow presumptuous; yes, it would be better to pay for his schooling, and now and then to send him some cast-off clothes. Then there was his other sister. Why, she had never done anything particular for him, so there was no reason why he should for her.

And his parents? It certainly would be his duty to allow them something, and he should do it. His father, as he heard from home, was getting very feeble, and could hardly earn five shillings a week by the chance work he did for the farmers, for he was past regular day-labor. His mother had been used to go out washing, but lately she had often been laid up with the rheumatism. A regular allowance should it be? Why, look what a sum horses and carriages cost; perhaps a present each quarter would be better; tea for his mother, and tobacco for his father. Yes, that would be better; his mother could make a little go a long way, and he would send a blanket also. No pledging himself to allowances; he might find that money would not go so far as he expected. Why, Squire Thorndike was always deep in debt, and he had four thousand a year. Sir Thomas Ludlow was known to be in difficulties, poor gentleman! He said free trade had made his means so small. Ah! free trade was a very hard thing; he should find it hard himself, when he had land, as of course he meant to have. He would send his parents something sometimes — not regularly — lest it should be supposed that he bound himself to continue it, which he might not be able to do. For of course he should have shares like other people in these railways — he might lose a great deal of money by them, as his master had done; he might by such means become quite poor again; and then how cruel it would seem to the old people to stop their money! He would send them something or other as soon as he knew himself what he was worth. Well, he was happy to say he had a generous mind, and did his duty to everybody that belonged to him.

Thus he sat and reflected till he had decided all this and more; he then peered through once more at his treasures, and having feasted his eyes sufficiently, contrived by means of a long stick to pull up two of the gold pieces. They were as large as silver crowns. He handled them, and turned them over. The whole, now he had part in his power, seemed doubly his own, but he knew that gold was heavy; he could count upwards of twenty of these bags; each, for aught he knew, might contain hundreds of gold pieces; and besides that, jewels glittered here and there, which he shrewdly suspected to be diamonds.

He heard voices at a distance, and hastened to emerge from his thicket of broom, first carefully putting the coins and a jewel in his waistcoat pocket. Covetousness grew stronger in his soul, and his breath came quick, and all his pulses throbbed with anxiety, lest he should not be able to secure and conceal the whole of the treasure for himself. The tourists returned, and Richard, as he followed them down the mountain, was so absorbed, that he was constantly treading on their heels. Afterwards, when he waited at table, his master thought the air must have intoxicated him, for he handed him powdered sugar to eat with his fish, salad with his gooseberry tart, and set a pat of butter on table with the dessert. Right glad was Richard when the work of the day was over, and he could retire to think upon his good fortune, and examine his spoils. They had been a very cumbersome possession to him, and had inspired him with an almost irresistible desire to be always feeling in his pocket to ascertain if they were safe, and a constant fear lest they should chink together and be heard.

Now, he thought, what must he do? Should he leave his master's service at once, buy some boxes, and, going up the mountain every day by himself, bring down by degrees the contents of that little cavern till all was secured? No, that would be a suspicious mode of proceeding; people would think the footman was mad, or, if he paid for what he wanted in ancient gold coins, they would suspect, watch, discover, and either betray him or insist upon sharing the spoils. He never doubted that there was a Lord of the Manor in those parts, and if so, he must be very secret, as of course these riches belonged of right to him.

No, it would not do to leave his master at once; far better to go south with him as far as the busy city of B——, where he was going to stay with a very learned old gentleman, a friend of his, who had a large collection of curiosities and dusty stones, shells, stuffed

animals, and other such gear. He should have a
great deal of leisure there, and B—— would be a
likely place to dispose of his coins in, for his master
would be busy with his friend tapping stones in the
country with tiny hammers, magnifying sand, and
bottling tadpoles in proof spirits.

Not to trouble my reader with accounts of how
Richard visited his treasures again by night, and in
coming down was very nearly discovered; how he
went again, and was very nearly falling over a preci-
pice; how he forgot his duties, was disrespectful, and
recklessly whistled as he followed his master; how
he entertained the project of shortly changing his
name, and conned 'The Peerage and Baronetage of
England' to find a grand and uncommon one; how
conveniently he thought this plan would hide him
from all those who had a claim upon him; how he
had compunctions on this head, and overcame them
with the thought of how much his poor relations would
expect of him if they knew about his riches; how the
landlady declared him to be the 'braggingest' young
man she had ever met with; how he carelessly neglected his master's luggage at B——, by reason where-
of it went down the line to London, and thence to
Dover; and how he spent the first two days of the
visit in staring out of the hall window,— I pass on to
say that never was there an old gentleman so fond of
old wood carving, old stained glass, old china, old
marbles, old mail, old books, old prints, old pictures,
and old coins, as this very old gentleman, this friend
of Richard's master.

On the third day Richard slipped out, and going

into a back street soon found a shop that he thought suited to his purpose. Here, after a little beating about the bush, he produced his coins and his diamond, and after a little hesitation on the part of the shopman, received eighteen guineas for the stone and one coin — far less than they were worth; but the man would not give more.

On returning, he was told that his master had been ringing for him; he ran upstairs in some trepidation, and found the two old gentlemen examining a large cabinet full of coins. 'Richard,' said his master, 'I want you to hold this tray.' Richard did so, and looked down on its contents. 'Those,' said the host to his friend, 'are early English.' He lifted up another light tray, and Richard held it on the top of the first. 'Now then, old fellow,' he exclaimed, 'this is something to be proud of indeed; Spanish coins — date of the Moors — all rare — this one, unique; I gave forty pounds for it.'

'Not a penny too much,' said Richard's master; 'and these two coins set apart — are they Spanish too?'

'Moorish, and all but unique; they've been in my family for generations.'

Richard looked down, and his heart beat so loud that he wondered they did not hear it; then he drew a long breath, and gazed intently, as well he might, for, reposing on cotton wool, side by side, were the very counterparts — the exact fac-similes — of the great gold pieces he got out of the cavern.

'What's the matter, Richard?' said his master; for Richard's hands shook, and he stared as if fascinated.

'Nothing's the matter, sir,' replied Richard, with a face of terror.

'I'll tell you what,' said the friend, when Richard had been dismissed, 'there's something queer about that lad; what does he mean by turning red and pale, and breathing as hard as if my coins had knocked the breath out of his body?'

His master also thought it queer when that same evening Richard gave him warning, and added that he wished to leave that night, for his brother's wife had written to say that her husband was dangerously ill, and wished to see him.

His master was vexed; but being an easy man, he paid Richard his wages, and let him go, with many kind wishes for his brother's recovery.

'And now,' said Richard, 'I'll be a gentleman. I've left my old clothes, and when I'm missed my family can claim them. Honest industry is the best thing after all. Let them do for themselves; they ought to be above troubling me; my name shall be Mr. Davenport St. Gilbert; I shall keep myself to myself, for I want nothing of them, and that alone will be a good thing for them, and more than they ever had reason to expect.'

He then went to a number of shops, and soon supplied himself with everything that he thought necessary to constitute him a gentleman — a handsome suit of clothes, studs, a new hat, a cane, and lastly a pair of gloves, which he had been very near forgetting; then he went to a hotel, ordered supper and a bed, and by seven o'clock the next morning was on his way to the Cumberland mountains. The image of that mountain was always present to his imagination, and the thought of the treasure lying there, with nothing but a little bird to watch it, filled him with a secret, sordid joy; it should be all his own — no other living man should touch one penny of it: poor Richard!

He went to an inn, ordered a good dinner and a bottle of wine. Alas! he was not used to port wine, and he thought as he paid for all, he would drink all. He did so, and the next day a racking headache made him glad to lie in bed till noon. He staid at that place another night, and, unhappily for him, repeated the folly of the previous one. It was not till the fourth day from his leaving B—— that he reached the end of his journey, and stepping out of a post-chaise found himself at the foot of the well-remembered Cumberland mountains.

He sauntered to the shore of the lake, and began to hurrah! with irrepressible exultation. He thought himself alone, but a dry cough behind him, and a finger laid on his shoulder, undeceived him. He turned round hastily, and beheld two policemen.

'What's your business, fellows?' he exclaimed, half angry, half afraid.

'*You're* our business,' was the reply. 'There's been a theft; you must come back with us to B——.'

'It's a lie, a base lie; it's a cruel lie,' cried Richard, frantically; 'there was no theft in the matter, the coin was my own.'

'Indeed! Well, young man, you needn't criminate yourself; how do you know we came after you about a coin? — it's no use stamping, nor crying either, you must come.'

The mountains and the lake swam before Richard's eye, as the two policemen took him between them, and walked him off to the railway station; he was frightened, but bewildered, and throughout the long journey he preserved a dogged silence, till at last the train arrived at B——, and there stood his master and the old gentleman waiting for him.

'This is the young fellow, sir, is'nt it?' inquired the policemen confidently.

'Yes,' said his master, in a tone of deep regret; 'I grieve to say it is.'

The next morning he was examined before a magistrate, but alas! during the night he had reflected that no one could prove his having stolen the coins (for on their account he never doubted that he had been arrested); he had also reflected that to tell the honest truth about them was most certainly to lose all; moreover, he had made up his mind that nothing worse than a month's imprisonment was at all likely to befall him, even if a case could be made out against him. He therefore resolved to run all risks, and declare that he had found the coins and the jewels in his father's potato-garden; he had turned them up with a hoe. How the time passed with Richard until his trial, I do not know, but his kind old master visited him frequently, and told him it would be his duty to give evidence against him.

Richard, however, persisted in his tale, though he became quieter and more fearful as the assizes drew near.

At length the eventful day of trial came on; his turn came; he felt guilty, though not of the crime imputed to him; and his anxiety increased as he listened to the evidence brought against him. The counsel for the prosecution stated the case against him thus:—

The prisoner, on the 22d of August, arrived with his master at the house of the prosecutor; he had often been there before, and was known to have acquaintances there. On the 24th he was present while certain valuable coins were displayed by the prosecutor; he was observed to regard them with particular attention; that same evening he gave warning to his master, giving as a reason that his brother's wife had written to him, declaring that her husband was at death's door. He requested to be paid his wages at once, alleging that he had but five shillings in his pocket. He took his leave; and in the evening of the following day, his brother, whose employer was travelling that way, called in to see him in perfect health; and on being told of the letter supposed to have been received from his wife, replied that his wife, being a Frenchwoman, lady's-maid in the family where he lived, could neither read nor write English, and that Richard knew that quite well.

The day after this, the prosecutor happened to observe a certain scratched appearance about the keyholes of two of his cabinets; he opened them hastily, and found every tray gone, with all their contents; in short, the whole case gutted. Inquiries were instantly set on foot, and plate to a considerable amount was also found to be missing; thereupon, the servants being examined, Richard's name was mentioned by all with suspicion. The cook deposed that during dinner, the day he left, Richard had inquired concerning the word 'unique.' 'Unique,' said the servants, 'means that no one has got such a coin except master;' to which he replied, 'If that's unique, they are no more unique than I am, and that I could prove to the present company if I chose.' The servants further deposed, that looking upon this as an idle boast, they had laughed at him, and dared him to produce one, and at last he had said that perhaps he might before he took his leave of them.

This evidence being important, the police had been set to work, and had discovered a fac-simile of the coin, of which only two specimens were supposed to be extant, exposed for sale in a shop window; they had also discovered that he had entered several shops, and spent money to an amount greatly exceeding his wages. The recovered coin being shown to the prosecutor, he challenged it, and produced a written description, wherein it was set forth that these ancient Spanish coins were supposed to be fresh from the Mint, and never to have passed into circulation.

The prisoner, on being arrested, had instantly mentioned these coins, and declared he came by them honestly. When examined before a magistrate, he declared that he had dug them up in his father's potato-garden. Search being made, another coin was found in his waistcoat pocket. On being told that the sharp outline of the coins proved that they had not been exposed to friction or damp, he added that he found them sealed up in an earthen pot.

On being asked how long it was since he had found them, he replied that it was while he lived in his late master's service. On being reminded by that gentleman that he had only visited his parents twice during that period, and that the first time they were paupers in the Union, and had no potato-garden, he replied that it was the second time; on being further reminded that during his second visit the ground was covered with a deep fall of snow, he refused to give any answer.

And now witnesses were called, and then followed the feeble defence of his own counsel. Richard was bewildered, but he perceived that the circumstantial evidence was so strong against him that nothing but the truth could save him, and the truth no man knew. He was brought in guilty, and sentenced to seven years' transportation.

Alas! what a casting down of his dream of riches! what a bitter disappointment for his covetous soul! He was sent back to prison, and there, when he had duly reflected on his position, he determined to purchase freedom by discovering the whole truth, and thus giving up his monopoly of the Moorish gold.

He sent for his master; he looked miserable, and as he sat on the bench in his prison-dress, with his face propped on his hands, he felt plainly that his master pitied him.

The old gentleman heard him to the end and made no comment, but he remained so long silent when the tale was finished, that Richard looked up surprised. 'Sir!' he exclaimed, 'surely you believe me now?'

'Alas, my poor fellow!' said his master, 'you have

told so many falsehoods, that it is no longer in my power to believe on the testimony of your lips, but only of my own senses; and this last story, Richard, seems to me the wildest of all. It will not serve you, nor delay your sentence one hour.'

'Yes, it will — indeed it will. O sir, sir, try me this once, and go and look behind those broom bushes.'

'Richard, you have a good father and mother, and good sisters, who are very, very poor, — if you had really found such a treasure, you would have contrived to send something to them.'

'I — I forgot them, sir,' faltered Richard.

'No, Richard,' said his master, with a sigh, 'you are a bad fellow, I'm afraid; but you're not so bad as that comes to. You have deceived me so often, that I'm not to be taken in any more.'

Richard protested, but his master would not believe his tale, and was about to take leave of him, when a bustle was heard outside the door, and his master's old friend appeared in a state of great excitement. He opened both hands, and in the palm of each was seen a coin, the very coins that had been missing. The real thieves had been detected, and, with very little delay, Richard was set at liberty.

'And now, sir, said he, ' come with me to the mountain, and see whether I spoke the truth.'

His master wondered greatly, but he went. They were within ten miles of the mountain, when a tremendous storm came on; the floods of rain and peals of thunder drove them into an inn for shelter, and there they staid during a long night of storm and tempest.

It was not till high noon that that terrible storm subsided; then as soon as it was safe to go abroad, Richard and his master set off on their mission. They went toiling up the same path that they had pursued before; the way was very rugged, for stones and earth had been dislodged by the storm.

'Richard,' said his master, 'we are nearly at the top of the mountain; surely we must have passed the place.'

They came down again, and the agitated Richard looked from right to left; all was so changed, so torn and disfigured, that he could not tell where he was. The tiny streams were tumbling torrents; the road was blocked with stones and rocks.

'Richard,' his master said again, 'we are nearly at the foot of the mountain; surely we have passed the place.'

His master went down to the inn. Richard continued to search: for three weary days he wandered up, and down, and about. Whether the force of the storm had driven rocks down, and filled up that little roofless room, or whether a torrent had defaced the place and concealed it, he could not tell; but certain it is he never found it; and from that day to this, no man's eyes have ever been gladdened with the sight of the Moorish gold.

He came to his master — 'Sir,' said he, 'the gold is not to be found, but I have had a great deal of time to consider, and I have come to think that my own greed has brought all this misery on me. Here's the two coins that I got of the treasure; let them go to my relations, for I'll have none of them, but try to win back my good character, for the loss of that has been worse than the loss of this gold.'

THE ONE-EYED SERVANT.

THE ONE-EYED SERVANT.

DO you see those two pretty cottages on opposite sides of the Common? How bright their windows are, and how prettily the vines trail over them! A year ago one of them was the dirtiest and most forlorn-looking place you can imagine, and its mistress the most untidy woman.

She was once sitting at her cottage door, with her arms folded, as if she were deep in thought, though, to look at her face, one would not have supposed she was doing more than idly watching the swallows as they floated about in the hot, clear air. Her gown was torn and shabby, her shoes down at heel; the little curtain in her casement, which had once been fresh and white, had a great rent in it; and altogether she looked poor and forlorn.

She sat some time, gazing across the common, when all on a sudden she heard a little noise, like stitching, near the ground. She looked down, and sitting on the border, under a wall-flower bush, she saw the funniest little man possible, with a blue coat, a yellow waistcoat, and red boots; he had got a small shoe on his lap, and he was stitching away at it with all his might.

'Good morning, mistress!' said the little man. 'A very fine day. Why may you be looking so earnestly across the common?'

'I was looking at my neighbor's cottage,' said the young woman.

'What! Tom, the gardener's wife?—little Polly, she used to be called; and a very pretty cottage it is, too! Looks thriving; doesn't it?'

'She was always lucky,' said Bella (for that was the young wife's name); 'and her husband is always good to her.'

'They were *both* good husbands at first,' interrupted the little cobbler, without stopping. 'Reach me my awl, mistress, will you, for you seem to have nothing to do: it lies close by your foot.'

'Well, I can't say but they were both very good husbands at first,' replied Bella, reaching the awl with a sigh; 'but mine has changed for the worse, and hers for the better; and then, look how she thrives. Only to think of our both being married on the same day; and now I've nothing, and she has two pigs, and a'—

'And a lot of flax that she spun in the winter,' interrupted the cobbler; 'and a Sunday gown, as good green stuff as ever was seen, and, to my knowledge, a handsome silk handkerchief for an apron; and a red waistcoat for her goodman, with three rows of blue glass buttons, and a flitch of bacon in the chimney, and a rope of onions.'

'O, she's a lucky woman!' exclaimed Bella.

'Ay, and a tea-tray, with Daniel in the lion's den

upon it,' continued the cobbler; 'and a fat baby in in the cradle.'

'O, I'm sure I don't envy her that last,' said Bella, pettishly. 'I've little enough for myself and my husband, letting alone children.'

'Why, mistress, isn't your husband in work?' asked the cobbler.

'No; he's at the ale-house.'

'Why, how's that? he used to be very sober. Can't he get work?'

'His last master wouldn't keep him, because he was so shabby.'

'Humph!' said the little man. 'He's a groom, is he not? Well, as I was saying, your neighbor opposite thrives; but no wonder! Well, I've nothing to do with other people's secrets; but I *could* tell you, only I'm busy, and must go.'

'Could tell me *what?*' cried the young wife. 'O good cobbler, don't go, for I've nothing to do. Pray tell me *why* it's no wonder that she should thrive.'

'Well,' said he, 'it's no business of mine, you know, but, as I said before, it's no wonder people thrive who have a servant — a hard-working one, too — who is always helping them.'

'A servant!' repeated Bella; 'my neighbor has a servant! No wonder, then, everything looks so neat about her; but I never saw this servant. I think you must be mistaken; besides, how could she afford to pay her wages?'

'She has a servant, I say,' repeated the cobbler — a one-eyed servant — but she pays her no wages, to my certain knowledge. Well, good morning, mistress, I must go.'

"Do stop one minute, cried Bella, urgently — 'where did she get this servant?'

'O, I don't know,' said the cobbler; 'servants are plentiful enough; and Polly uses hers well, I can tell you.'

'And what does she do for her?'

'Do for her? Why, all sorts of things — I think she's the cause of her prosperity. To my knowledge she never refuses to do anything — keeps Tom's and Polly's clothes in beautiful order, and the baby's.'

'Dear me!' said Bella, in an envious tone, and holding up both her hands; 'well, she *is* a lucky woman, and I always said so. She takes good care *I* shall never see her servant. What sort of a servant is she, and how came she to have only one eye?'

'It runs in her family,' replied the cobbler, stitching busily, 'they are all so — one eye apiece; yet they make a very good use of it, and Polly's servant has four cousins who are blind — stone-blind; no eyes at all; and they sometimes come and help her. I've seen them in the cottage myself, and that's how Polly gets a good deal of her money. They work for her, and she takes what they make to market, and buys all those handsome things.'

'Only think,' said Bella, almost ready to cry with vexation, 'and I've not got a soul to do anything for *me;* how hard it is!' and she took up her apron to wipe away her tears.

The cobbler looked attentively at her. 'Well, you

are to be pitied, certainly,' he said, ' and if I were not in such a hurry ' —

' O, do go on, pray — were you going to say *you* could help me? I've heard that your people are fond of curds and whey, and fresh gooseberry syllabub. Now, if you would help me, trust me that there should be the most beautiful curds and whey set every night for you on the hearth; and nobody should ever look when you went and came.'

' Why, you see,' said the cobbler, hesitating, ' my people are extremely particular about — in short, about — cleanliness, mistress; and your house is not what one would call very clean. No offence, I hope?'

Bella blushed deeply. ' Well, but it should be always clean if you would — every day of my life I would wash the floor, and sand it, and the hearth should be whitewashed as white as snow, and the windows cleaned.'

' Well,' said the cobbler, seeming to consider, ' well, then, I should not wonder if I could meet with a one-eyed servant for you, like your neighbor's; but it may be several days before I can; and mind, mistress, I'm to have a dish of curds.'

' Yes, and some whipped cream, too,' replied Bella, full of joy.

The cobbler then took up all his tools, wrapped them in his leather apron, walked behind the wall-flower, and disappeared.

Bella was so delighted, she could not sleep that night for joy. Her husband scarcely knew the house, she had made it so bright and clean; and by night she had washed the curtain, cleaned the window, rubbed the fire-irons, sanded the floor, and set a great jug of hawthorn in blossom on the hearth.

The next morning Bella kept a sharp look-out both for the tiny cobbler and on her neighbor's house, to see whether she could possibly catch a glimpse of the one-eyed servant. But, no — nothing could she see but her neighbor sitting on her rocking-chair, with her baby on her knee, working.

At last, when she was quite tired, she heard the voice of the cobbler outside. She ran to the door, and cried out, —

'O, do, pray, come in, sir; only look at my house!'

'Really,' said the cobbler, looking round, 'I declare I should hardly have known it — the sun can shine brightly now through the clear glass; and what a sweet smell of hawthorn!'

'Well, and my one-eyed servant?' asked Bella — 'you remember, I hope, that I can't pay her any wages — have you met with one that will come?'

'All's right,' replied the little man, nodding. 'I've got her with me.'

'Got her with you?' repeated Bella, looking round; 'I see nobody.'

'Look, here she is!' said the cobbler, holding up something in his hand.

Would you believe it? the one-eyed servant was nothing but a Needle.

THE GOLDEN OPPORTUNITY.

NOT many things have happened to me in the course of my life which can be called events. One great event, as I then thought it, happened when I was eight years old. On that birthday I first possessed a piece of gold.

How well I remember the occasion! I had a holiday, and was reading aloud to my mother. The book was the 'Life of Howard, the philanthropist.' I was interested in it, though the style was considerably above my comprehension; at last I came to the following sentence, which I could make nothing of: 'He could not let slip such a golden opportunity for doing good.'

'What is a golden opportunity?' I inquired.

'It means a very good opportunity.'

'But, mamma, why do they call it *golden*?'

My mamma smiled, and said it was a figurative expression: 'Gold is very valuable and very uncommon; this opportunity was a very valuable and uncommon one; we can express that in one word, by calling it a golden opportunity.'

I pondered upon the information for some time, and

then made a reply to the effect, that all the golden opportunities seemed to happen to very rich people, or people who lived a long time ago, or else to great men, whose lives we can read in books — very great men, such as Wilberforce and Howard; but they never happened to *real* people, whom we could see every day, nor to children.'

'To children like you, Orris?' said my mother; 'why, what kind of a golden opportunity are you wishing for just now?'

My reply was childish enough.

'If I were a great man I should like to sail after the slave ships, fight them, and take back the poor slaves to their own country. Or I should like to do something like what Quintus Curtius did. Not exactly like that; because you know, mamma, if I were to jump into a gulf, that would not really make it close.'

'No,' said my mother, 'it would not.'

'And besides,' I reasoned, 'if it *had* closed, I should never have known of the good I had done, because I should have been killed.'

'Certainly,' said my mother; I saw her smile, and thinking it was at the folly of my last wish, hastened to bring forward a wiser one.

'I think I should like to be a great lady, and then if there had been a bad harvest, and all the poor people on my lord's land were nearly starving, I should like to come down to them with a purse full of money, and divide it among them. But you see, mamma, I *have* no golden opportunities.'

'My dear, we all have some opportunities for doing

good, and they are golden, or not, according to the use we make of them.'

'But, mamma, we cannot get people released out of prison, as Howard did.'

'No; but sometimes, by instructing them in their duty, by providing them with work, so that they shall earn bread enough, and not be tempted, and driven by hunger to steal, we can prevent some people from being ever put in prison.'

My mother continued to explain that those who really desired to do good never wanted opportunities, and that the difference between Howard and other people was more in perseverance and earnestness than in circumstances. But I do not profess to remember much of what she said; I only know that, very shortly, she took me into my grandfather's study, and sitting down, began busily to mend a heap of pens which lay beside him on the table.

He was correcting proof-sheets, and, knowing that I must not talk, I stood awhile very quietly watching him.

Presently I saw him mark out a letter in the page, make a long stroke in the margin, and write a letter *d* beside it.

Curiosity was too much for my prudence; I could not help saying—

'Grandpapa, what did you write that letter *d* for?'

'There was a letter too much in the word, child,' he replied; '*I* spell "potatoes" with only one *p*, and want the printer to put out the second.'

'Then *d* stands for *don't*, I suppose, was my next observation; 'it means don't put it in.'

'Yes, child, yes; something like that.'

If it had not been my birthday I should not have had courage to interrupt him again. 'But, grandpapa, "*do*" begins with *d*, so how is the printer to know whether you mean "do," or "don't?"'

My grandfather said 'Pshaw!' turned short round upon my mother, and asked her if she had heard what I said?

My mother admitted that it was a childish observation.

'Childish!' repeated my grandfather, 'childish! she'll never be anything but a child — never; she has no reasoning faculties at all.' When my grandfather was displeased with me, he never scolded me for the fault of the moment, but inveighed against me *in the piece*, as a draper would say.

'Did *you* ever talk nonsense at her age — ever play with a penny doll, and sing to a kitten? I should think not.'

'I was of a different disposition,' said my mother, gently.

'Ay,' said the old man, 'that you were. Why, I wouldn't trust this child, as I trusted you, for the world; you were quite a little woman, could pay bills, or take charge of keys; but this child has no discretion — no head-piece. She says things that are wide of the mark. She's — well, my dear, I didn't mean to vex you — she's a nice child enough, but, bless me, she never *thinks*, and never reasons about any thing.'

He was mistaken. I was thinking and reasoning at that moment. I was thinking how delightful it would be if I might have the cellar keys, and all the other keys hanging to my side, so that every one might see that I was trusted with them; and I was reasoning, that perhaps my mother had behaved like a little woman, because she was treated like one.

'My dear, I did not mean that she was worse than many other children,' repeated my grandfather; 'come here, child, and I'll kiss you.'

My mother pleaded, by way of apology for me,— 'She has a very good memory.'

'Memory! ay, there's another disadvantage. She remembers everything; she's a mere parrot. Why, when you, at her age, wanted a punishment, if I set you twenty lines of poetry, they'd keep you quiet for an hour. Set this child eighty — knows 'em directly, and there's time wasted in hearing her say 'em into the bargain.'

'I hope she will become more thoughtful as she grows older,' said my mother, gently.

'I hope she will; there's room for improvement. Come and sit on my knee, child. So this is your birthday. Well, I suppose I must give you some present or other. Leave the child with me, my dear, I'll take care of her. But I won't detain you, for the proofs are all ready. Open the door for your mother, Orris. Ah! you'll never be anything like her — never.'

I did as he desired, and then my grandfather, looking at me with comical gravity, took out a leathern purse, and dived with his fingers among the contents. 'When I was a little boy, as old as you are, nobody gave *me* any money.'

Encouraged by his returning good humor, I drew

closer and peeped into the purse. There were as many as six or eight sovereigns in it. I thought what a rich man my grandfather was, and when he took out a small coin and laid it on my palm, I could scarcely believe it was for me.

'Do you know what that is, child?'

'A half-sovereign, grandpapa.'

'Well, do you think you could spend it?'

'O, yes, grandpapa.'

'"O, yes!" and she opens her eyes! Ah, child, child! that money was worth ten shillings when it was in my purse, and I wouldn't give sixpence for anything it will buy, now it has once touched your little fingers.'

'Did you give it me to spend exactly as I like, grandpapa?'

'To be sure, child — there, take it — it's worth nothing to you, my dear.'

'Nothing to me! The half-sovereign worth nothing to me! why, grandpapa?'

'Nothing worth mentioning; you have no real wants; you have clothes, food, and shelter, without this half-sovereign.'

'O, yes; but, grandpapa, I think it must be worth ten times as much to me as to you; I have only this one, and you have quantities; I shouldn't wonder if you have thirty or forty half-sovereigns, and a great many shillings and half-crowns besides, to spend every year.'

'I shouldn't wonder!'

'And I have only one. I can't think, grandpapa, what you do with all your money; if I had it I would buy so many delightful things with it.'

'No doubt! kaleidoscopes, and magic lanterns, and all sorts of trash. But, unfortunately, you have not got it; you have only one half-sovereign to throw away.'

'But perhaps I shall not throw it away; perhaps I shall try and do some good with it.'

'Do some good with it! Bless you, my dear, if you do but try to do some good with it, I shall not call it thrown away.'

I then related what I had been reading, and had nearly concluded when the housemaid came in. She laid a crumpled piece of paper by his desk, and with it a shilling and a penny, saying. 'There's the change, sir, out of your shoemaker's bill.'

My grandfather took it up, looked at it, and remarked that the shilling was a new one. Then with a generosity which I really am at a loss to account for, he actually, and on the spot, gave me both the shilling and the penny.

There they lay in the palm of my hand, gold, silver, and copper. He then gave me another kiss, and abruptly dismissed me, saying that he had more writing to do; and I walked along the little passage with an exultation of heart that a queen might have envied, to show this unheard-of wealth to my mother.

I remember laying the three coins upon a little table, and dancing round it, singing, 'There's a golden opportunity! and there's a silver opportunity! and there's a copper opportunity!' and having continued this exercise till I was quite tired, I spent the rest of the morning in making three little silk bags, one for each of them, previously rubbing the penny with sand-paper, to make it bright and clean.

Visions and dreams floated through my brain as to the good I was to do with this property. They were vainglorious but not selfish; but they were none of them fulfilled, and need not be recorded. The next day, just as my lessons were finished, papa came in with his hat and stick in his hand; he was going to walk to the town, and offered to take me with him.

It was always a treat to walk out with my father, especially when he went to the town. I liked to look in at the shop windows, and admire their various contents.

To the town therefore we went. My father was going to the Mechanics' Institute, and could not take me in with him, but there was a certain basket-maker, with whose wife I was often left on these occasions. To this good woman he brought me, and went away, promising not to be long.

And now, dear reader, whoever you may be, I beseech you judge not too harshly of me; remember I was but a child, and it is certain that if you are not a child yourself, there was a time when you were one. Next door to the basket-maker's there was a toy-shop, and in its window I espied several new and very handsome toys.

'Mr. Miller's window looks uncommon gay,' said the old basket-maker, observing the direction of my eyes.

'Uncommon,' repeated his wife; 'those new gimcracks from London is handsome sure-ly.'

'Wife,' said the old man, 'there's no harm in missy's just taking a look at 'em — eh?'

'Not a bit in the world,' bless her,' said the old woman; 'I know she'll go no further, and come back here when she's looked 'em over.'

'O, yes, indeed I will. Mrs. Stebbs, may I go?'

The old woman nodded assent, and I was soon before the window.

Splendid visions! O, the enviable position of Mr. Miller! How wonderful that he was not always playing with his toys, showing himself his magic lanterns, setting out his puzzles, and winding up his musical boxes! Still more wonderful, that he could bear to part with them for mere money!

I was lost in admiration when Mr. Miller's voice made me start. 'Wouldn't you like to step inside, miss?'

He said this so affably that I felt myself quite welcome, and was beguiled into entering. In an instant he was behind the counter. 'What is the little article I can have the pleasure, miss' —

'O!' I replied, blushing deeply, 'I do not want to buy anything this morning, Mr. Miller.'

'Indeed, miss, that's *rather* a pity. I'm sorry, miss, I confess, on *your* account. I should like to have served you, while I have goods about me that I'm proud of. In a week or two,' and he looked pompously about him, 'I should say in less time than that, they'll all be cleared out.'

'What! will they all be gone — all sold?' I exclaimed in dismay.

'Just so, miss; such is the appreciation of the public;' and he carelessly took up a little cedar stick and played 'The Blue Bells of Scotland' on the glass keys of a plaything piano.

'This,' he observed, coolly throwing down the stick and taking up an accordion, 'this delightful little instrument is half-a-guinea — equal to the finest notes of the hautboy.' He drew it out, and in his skilful hands it 'discoursed' music, which I thought the most excellent I had ever heard.

But what is the use of minutely describing my temptation? In ten minutes the accordion was folded up in silver paper, and I had parted with my cherished half-sovereign.

As we walked home, I enlarged on the delight I should have in playing on my accordion. 'It is so easy, papa; you have only to draw it in and out; I can even play it at dinner-time, if you like, between the meat and the puddings. You know the queen has a band, papa, to play while she dines, and so can you.'

My father abruptly declined this liberal offer; so did my grandfather, when I repeated it to him, but I was relieved to find that he was not in the least surprised at the way in which I had spent his present. This, however, did not prevent my feeling sundry twinges of regret when I remembered all my good intentions. But, alas! my accordion soon cost me tears of bitter disappointment. Whether from its fault, or my own, I could not tell, but draw it out, and twist it about as I might, it would not play 'The Blue Bells of Scotland,' or any other of my favorite tunes. It was just like the piano, every tune must be learned;

there was no music inside which only wanted winding out of it, as you wind the tunes out of barrel organs.

My mother, coming in some time during that melancholy afternoon, found me sitting at the foot of my little bed holding my accordion, and shedding over it some of the most bitter tears that shame and repentance had yet wrung from me.

She looked astonished, and asked, 'What is the matter, my child?'

'O, mamma,' I replied, as well as my sobs would let me, 'I have bought this thing which won't play, and I have given Mr. Miller my golden opportunity.'

'What, have you spent your half-sovereign? I thought you were going to put poor little Patty Morgan to school with it, and give her a new frock and tippet.'

My tears fell afresh at this, and I thought how pretty little Patty would have looked in the new frock, and that I should have put it on for her myself. My mother sat down by me, took away the toy, and dried my eyes. 'Now you see, my child,' she observed, 'one great difference between those who are earnestly desirous to do good, and those who only wish it lightly. You *had* what you were wishing for—a good opportunity; for a child like you, an unusual opportunity for doing good. You had the means of putting a poor little orphan to school for one whole year—think of that, Orris! In one whole year she might have learned a great deal about the God who made her, and who gave His Son to die for her, and His Spirit to make her holy. One whole year would have gone a great way towards teaching her to read the Bible; in one year she might have learned a great many hymns, and a great many useful things, which would have been of service to her when she was old enough to get her own living. And for what have you thrown all this good from you and from her?'

'I am very, very sorry. I did not mean to buy the accordion: I forgot, when I heard Mr. Miller playing upon it, that I had better not listen; and I never remembered what I had done till it was mine, and folded up in paper.'

'You forgot till it was too late?'

'Yes, mamma; but, O, I am so sorry. I am sure I shall never do so any more.'

'Do not say so, my child; I fear it will happen again, many, many times.'

'Many times? O mamma! I will never go into Mr. Miller's shop again.'

'My dear child, do you think there is nothing in the world that can tempt you but Mr. Miller's shop?'

'Even if I go there,' I sobbed, in the bitterness of my sorrow, 'it will not matter now, for I have now no half-sovereign left to spend; but if I had another, and he were to show me the most beautiful toys in the world, I would not buy them after this—not if they would play of themselves.'

'My dear, that may be true; you, perhaps, would not be tempted again when you were on your guard; but you know, Orris, you do not wish for another toy of that kind. Are there no temptations against which you are not on your guard?'

I thought my mother spoke in a tone of sorrow. I

knew she lamented my volatile disposition; and crying afresh, I said to her, 'O, mamma, do you think that all my life I shall never do any good at all?'

'If you try in your own strength, I scarcely think you will. Certainly you will do no good which will be acceptable to God.'

'Did I try in my own strength to-day?'

'What do you think, Orris? I leave it to you to decide.'

'I am afraid I did.'

'I am afraid so too; but you must not cry and sob in this way. Let this morning's experience show you how open you are to temptation. To let it make you think you shall never yield to such temptation again is the worst thing you can do; you need help from above; seek it, my dear child, otherwise all your good resolutions will come to nothing.'

'And if I do seek it, mamma?'

'Then, weak as you are, you will certainly be able to accomplish something. It is impossible for me to take away your volatile disposition, and make you thoughtful and steady; but "with God all things are possible."'

'It is a great pity that at the very moment when I want to think about right things, and good things, all sorts of nonsense comes into my head. Grandpapa says I am just like a whirligig; and, besides, that I can never help laughing when I ought not, and I am always having lessons set me for running about and making such a noise when baby is asleep.'

'My dear child, you must not be discontented, these are certainly disadvantages; they will give you a great deal of trouble, and myself, too; but you have one advantage that all children are not blessed with.'

'What is that, mamma?'

'There are times when you sincerely wish to do good.'

'Yes, I think I really do, mamma; I had better fold up this thing, and put it away, for it only vexes me to see it. I am sorry I have lost my golden opportunity.'

And so, not without tears, the toy was put away. The silver and the copper remained, but there was an end of my golden opportunity.

My birth-day had been gone by a week, and still the shilling and the penny lay folded in their silken shrines.

I had quite recovered my spirits, and was beginning to think how I should spend them, particularly the shilling, for I scarcely thought any good could be done with such a small sum as a penny. Now there was a poor Irish boy in our neighborhood, who had come with the reapers, and been left behind with a hurt in his leg.

My mother had often been to see him. While he was confined to his bed, she went regularly to read with him, and sometimes she sent me with our nurse-maid to take him a dinner.

He was now much better, and could get about a little. To my mother's surprise she found that he could read perfectly well. One day, when she met him, he 'thanked her honor for all favors,' and said he should soon be well enough to return to old Ireland.

As we walked home one day my mother said to

me, 'Orris, if you like, I will tell you of a good way to spend your shilling. You may buy poor Tim a Testament.'

I was delighted, and gave my immediate assent.

'Well, then,' said my mother, 'that is settled. I should have given one myself to Tim, if you had wished to spend your shilling in something else. And now, remember, you must not change your mind; papa is going to the town to-morrow, you may go with him and get one then.'

To-morrow came, and with it a note to me from my two cousins, saying that they were coming over to spend the afternoon with me, and see my Indian corn, and my tobacco plants, which I had planted myself.

I was very proud of my corn, and still more proud that my cousins should think it worth while to come and see it, for they were three or four years older than myself, and did not often take part in my amusements.

By dint of great industry I finished my lessons an hour earlier than usual, and ran into the garden to see how my corn looked. Old gardener himself admitted that it was beautiful; the glossy, green leaves fell back like silken streamers, and displayed the grain with its many shades of green, gold, and brown.

I thought how delightful it would be if I could build a kind of bower over against it, in which my cousins could sit and admire it at their leisure. There were some hop plants growing just in the right place; I had only to untwist them; and there was a clematis that could easily be pressed into the service.

I set to work, and, with a little help from gardener, soon made two or three low arches, over which I carefully trained the flowering hops, and mingled them with festoons of clematis. The bower seemed to be worthy of a queen at the least; and no doubt it was really pretty.

I was just carrying some pots of balsams in flower to set at the entrance, when my father came up. 'Well, Orris,' he said, 'mamma tells me you want to go to the town. Be quick if you do, for I am just ready to start.'

'Just ready! O, papa, surely it is not one o'clock? If I go this bower will never be finished by three.'

'Certainly not, we shall scarcely be home by three; but why need it be finished?'

'Don't you remember, papa, that Elsy and Anne are coming?'

'O, I had forgotten that important fact. Well, then, if they are to sit in this bower, I think you must stay at home and finish it; you can go with me some other day.'

Now my father knew nothing about the Testament, or he would doubtless have given different advice. While I hesitated, anxious to stay, and yet afraid not to go, my mother drew near, and I thought I would leave it to her to decide.

'The child wants to finish her bower, my dear,' said my father, 'therefore, as it is not particularly convenient to me to have her to-day, she may stay at home if she likes, for, I presume, her errand is of no great consequence.'

My mother made no answer; in another moment

he was gone, and I was left with a long hop tendril in my hand, and a face flushed with heat and agitation.

I thought my mother would speak, and advise me to run after my father, but she did not; and I went on with my work, conscious that her eyes were upon me.

Presently, to my great relief, gardener came up, and asked her some questions about the flower-beds. She went away with him, and I breathed more freely, comforting myself with the thought that I could easily buy the Testament another day.

I worked faster than ever, partly to drive away reproachful thoughts. The little bower was lovely, it was scarcely high enough for me to stand upright in, but it would be delightful I knew for us to sit under. Gardener had been mowing, and when I had brought a quantity of sun-dried grass, and spread it thickly over the floor, I thought my bower an eighth wonder of the world. My cousins came shortly, and confirmed me in this opinion; they spent a very happy afternoon, seated under it; and, but for remembering the Irish boy, I might have been happy also. We were very quiet till after tea, and then I am sorry to say that our high spirits quite carried us away; we got into mischief, and my share of it was throwing an apple into the greenhouse, and breaking two panes of glass. This was on a Saturday.

On Sunday no one mentioned either this or the Irish boy; but on Monday, just as I had finished my lessons, I saw my father pass the window, and ventured to ask mamma if he was going to the town, and whether I might walk with him.

'Why do you wish to go, Orris?' she inquired.

'To buy the Testament, mamma, for poor Tim.'

'He is gone, said my mother; 'he went away early this morning.'

I put on my garden bonnet, and went out, with a curious sensation, as if, when I did wrong, all circumstances conspired to punish me. I turned the corner of the greenhouse, and there stood my father, looking at the broken panes.

'Orris,' he said, 'did you do this mischief?'

'Yes, papa.'

'This is the third time it has happened. I have repeatedly forbidden you to play in this part of the garden.'

'I am very sorry, papa.'

'Your sorrow will not mend the glass, and I am afraid it will not make you more obedient another time.'

He spoke so gravely, that I knew he really was displeased. After a pause, he said, —

'Have you got any money?'

'I have a shilling, papa, and a penny.'

'It will cost more than that to repair this damage; I shall be obliged to claim forfeit of the shilling.'

I wiped away two or three tears, and produced my little silk bag; he turned it over, and bit his lips; perhaps its elaborate workmanship made him understand that a shilling was much more for me to give up than for him to receive.

'Is this all you have got?' he inquired.

'Excepting the penny, papa,' I replied; and, child as I was, I perfectly understood his vexation at having to take it from me. He remained so long looking at it as it lay in his palm, that I even hoped he would return it, and say he would excuse me that once. But no, he was too wise; he put it at last into his waistcoat pocket, and walked away, saying, 'I hope this will make you more careful another time.'

He went towards the house, and I watched him till he entered. Then I ran to my bower, sat down upon the dried grass, and began to cry as if my heart would break.

Repentance and regret, though they may be keenly felt by a child, are not reasoned on very distinctly. I had often been very sorry before, but whether for the fault, as distinct from the punishment, I had scarcely inquired. I was heartily sorry now, not only for my disobedience, and because my father had forfeited the shilling, but because I saw it had vexed and hurt him to do it — not only because I had preferred pleasure to duty, neglected the opportunity for doing good, and lost it — but because the feeling, if not the words of St. Paul pressed heavily upon my heart: 'When I would do good, evil is present with me.'

I was still crying, when, on a sudden, looking up, I saw my father standing before me, and watching me with evident regret. My first impulse was to say, 'O, papa, I was not crying about the shilling.'

He beckoned me to rise out of my bower, and said, 'Then what were you crying about, my little darling?'

I tried not to sob; he led me to a garden seat and took me on his knee; then, with a great many tears, I told him all that I have now been telling you, and ended with a passion of crying. O, papa, do teach me to be different, and to wish the same thing when I am tempted, that I do when no pleasure tempts me. Pray teach me to do good.'

'My dear child, God is teaching you now.'

'What, papa? when my golden opportunity is gone, and my silver opportunity has come to nothing?'

'Quite true; but then you are doubly sure now, you know by ample experience, do you not — that of yourself you can do nothing?'

I was so convinced of it, that I was verging on an opposite fault of self-confidence. I was almost doubting whether any assistance that I could hope to have would make me proof against temptation.

But now was my father's 'golden opportunity,' and he availed himself of it. Although I cannot remember his words, their influence remains to this day. Certain sensations and impressions connected with that wise and fatherly conversation return upon me often, even now. It conveyed to my mind the idea that this weakness itself was to be my strength, if it made me depend upon a stronger than myself; that this changeable disposition would make more precious to me the knowledge that 'with God is no variableness, neither shadow of changing.'

When he ceased to speak, I said, with a sorrowful sigh, 'And now, papa, there is only one penny left of all my opportunities!'

'Well, my darling,' he replied, 'it is possible that you may do acceptable good even with that. Remember what our Saviour said about the cup of cold water.'

'Yes,' I said; 'but the person who gave the cold

water had nothing better to give; he had not a cup of milk, or a cup of wine, which he first wasted and threw away.'

'My dear, you need not inquire into that; you might have done better; but as there it still something to be done, "do it with thy might."'

When I was quite calm again, and almost happy, he sent me into the house to play at ball. As I passed the kitchen door, a poor old woman, whom my mother used sometimes to help, turned from it, and I heard the housemaid say, 'Mistress has just walked out, and I cannot say when she will be at home.'

She was hobbling away, when I bethought me of my penny, took it out of its bag, and pulling her by the cloak, offered it to her.

At first she did not seem to understand me, but when she saw my copper opportunity, which was as bright as sand-paper could render it, she gave me just the shadow of a smile, and taking it in her skinny hand, said, 'I thank you kindly, my pretty.'

'Poor old creature,' said the housemaid, 'that will buy her a trifle, mayhap; she and her husband are going into the workhouse to-morrow.'

I passed into the house penniless, but in a subdued and humble state of mind. The lessons I had had were not without good effect; but it cannot be expected that I can remember much of the working of my mind. I only know that time *did* pass; that I went to bed, got up, said my lessons, and had my play for a long time, perhaps a fortnight. At the end of about that time my little sister Sophy and I went out one day for a long walk with Matilda, our nurse, and took a basket with us to put flowers in, and blackberries, if we should be so fortunate as to find any.

We walked a long way till Sophy was tired, and became clamorous to sit down; so Matilda led us to the entrance of a wood, and there we sat and rested on the steps of a stile. There was a cottage near at hand; presently an old woman came out with a kettle in her hand, and I recognized her as the woman to whom I had given my penny. She hobbled to the edge of a little stream which flowed close to our seat, and dipped her kettle in, but did not notice us till Matilda called her.

'How are you, Mrs. Grattan, and how's your old gentleman?'

'Thank you kindly, girl, we be pretty moderate,' was the reply. 'He,' and she pointed with her stick to a field opposite, where several men were at work, '*he* be among them picking up stones — ha! ha! He be as blithe as a boy.'

'We was all very glad up at the Grange to hear of your good luck,' said Matilda, in the loudest tones of her cheerful voice, for the old woman was rather deaf. 'Our mistress was main glad, I'll assure you.'

'Ah! very kind on you all. How be the old gentleman?'

'Quite hearty.'

By this time she had reached us, set down her kettle, and taken her place beside Matilda. I was busily plaiting straw, but I listened carelessly to their conversation.

'And so you got your rent paid and all,' said Ma-

tilda, turning her eager black eyes on the old woman.
'What a good son Joe is to you!'

'Ah, that he be, dear,' was the reply; 'that he be; wrote he did, so pretty, "My dear mother," he says, "don't you go for to think I shall ever forget how good you was to me always, for I shall not," he says'—

Matilda's eyes flashed and glistened; she took a particular interest in this young man, though I did not know that till long afterwards.

'Tell us how it all was!' she said, quickly.

'Why, you see, dear, he was not my own, but I did as well as I could by him; and he be as fond of me like, ay, fonder, than he be of his father.'

'Yes, I know,' said Matilda.

'Well, dear, I went to Mr. T.'s house' (my father's), 'and I was very down at heart—very, I was; for Mr. Ball, he'd been that morning, and says he, "It signifies nothing that you've lived here so long," he says, "if you can't pay the rent." I says, "Mr. Ball, will you please to consider these weeks and weeks that my poor old man has been laid up wi' rheumatize." "But," he says, "I can put in younger and stronger than him; and besides that," he says, "I know you owe money at the shop, over all you owe to my employer."'

'He was always a hard man,' said Matilda.

'Well, dear, he says, "It ain't no use my deceiving of you, Mrs. Grattan, but I must sell you up, for," says he, "the money I must have, and you must go into the workhouse; it's the best place by half for such as you." And, dear, it seemed hard, for,' I'll assure you, we hadn't a half-ounce of tea, nor a lump of coal in the house, for we was willing, my old man and me, to strive to the last to pay our owings, and we was living very hard.'

'How much did you owe?' asked Matilda.

'Over three pounds, dear; and then the rent was four. I hadn't one half-penny in the house; I paid the baker Thursday was a week; t'other four was for the doctor, and we was hungry and cold, we was; but the Lord be praised, we ain't now.'

'Ah! Joe's a good son.'

'As good as ever breathed, dear; but we hadn't heard from him of a long while, by reason his regiment was up the country, but you'll understand I didn't know that till I got his letter. And so we was to be sold up, and go into the House. I fretted a deal, and then I thought I'd go and tell your missis — she be a good friend. But deary me! I owed such a world o' money; only, thinks I, she'll be main sorry to hear we must go, and a body likes somebody to be sorry.'

'Ah! to be sure they do,' said Matilda.

'But she was out, and so I got nothing, only this child, bless her! she runs up and gives me a penny; but, deary me, thinks I, what's a penny to them as owes £7, 2s. But, thinks I, my old man and me, we won't cry together in the dark this last night; so I walked on to the town with it to buy a half-penny candle of Mr. Sims at the post-office. I was half way there from my place, and when I got into the shop, "Sit you down, Mrs. Grattan," says he, for he saw I was main tired; "I haven't seen you of a long time."

'"And that's true, Mr. Sims," says I, "for it's little enough I have to lay out, and the shop t'other side of the turnpike be nigher."

'Well, I sat me down; maybe a quarter of an hour after I'd bought my candle, and just as I was a-going, in comes Mrs. Sims, and, says she, "Is that Grattan's wife?"

'"Ay," says he.

'"Well," says she, "I reckon you remembered to give her that letter."

'"A good thing you spoke, my dear," says he, "I should have forgot it — that I should."

'If you'll believe me, I trembled like a leaf, to think I should so near have missed it. "Be it a letter from the Indies?" says I.

'"Ay," says he, "that it is, and nothing to pay on it; and it's marked, 'To be left at the post-office till called for.'"

'Well, dear, I took it home, and waited for my old man to come home, by reason I can't read, and about dusk he comes in, and we lights the candle, and my old man he read it right out, for he's a fine scholar. And there was two five-pound notes inside, bless him; and he says, "Mother, I've got made sergeant, and now I shall send to you regular."'

'Well, I've heard no better news this many a day!' said Matilda.

'It *was* good, dear. Well, I paid the doctor, and when Mr. Ball came next day, says I, "There's the money, sir," and he stared. "Indeed," he says; "I am surprised, but them that pay can stay." So, you see, there's money to spend, more money, dear, when we be laid up with the rheumatize." Upon this she laughed with genuine joy, and, taking up her kettle, wished Matilda good afternoon, and hobbled away.

And I knew, though it had never occurred to the old woman, that all this happiness was owing to my penny! If she had not had it to spend, she would not have walked to the post-office, she would not have got her son's letter — that precious letter which had saved her from misery and the workhouse.

How happy I was as we walked home; I seemed to tread on air, and yet I knew of how little value the penny really was; it was only my having been permitted to give it under such peculiar circumstances that had made it such a worthy and important coin.

The lesson taught me by these little events I did not easily forget, and I think their moral is too obvious to need elaborate enforcing. It may, however, be summed up in few words.

First, — Do not expect that in your own strength you can make use of even the best opportunity for doing good.

Second, — Do not put off till another day any good which it is in the power of your hand to do at once.

And *thirdly*, — Do not despond because your means of doing good appear trifling and insignificant, for though one soweth and another reapeth, yet it is God that giveth the increase; and who can tell whether He will not cause that which is sown to bear fruit an hundred fold; who can tell whether to have even a penny to give under certain circumstances may not be to have no Copper — but a Golden Opportunity.

THE WILD-DUCK SHOOTER.

THE charity of the rich is much to be commended, but how beautiful is the charity of the poor!
Call to mind the coldest day you ever experienced. Think of the bitter wind and driving snow; think how you shook and shivered — how the sharp white particles were driven up against your face — how, within doors, the carpets were lifted like billows along the floors, the wind howled and moaned in the chimneys, windows creaked, doors rattled, and every now and then heavy lumps of snow came thundering down with a dull weight from the roof.

Now hear my story.

In one of the broad, open plains of Lincolnshire, there is a long, reedy sheet of water, a favorite resort of wild ducks. At its northern extremity stand two mud cottages, old and out of repair.

One bitter, bitter night, when the snow lay three feet deep on the ground, and a cutting east wind was driving it about, and whistling in the dry frozen reeds by the water's edge, and swinging the bare willow trees till their branches swept the ice, an old woman sat spinning in one of these cottages before a moderately cheerful fire. Her kettle was singing on the coals; she had a reed-candle, or home-made rushlight on her table, but the full moon shone in, and was the brighter light of the two. These two cottages were far from any road, or any other habitation; the old woman was, therefore, surprised, as she sat drawing out her thread, and crooning an old north-country song, to hear a sudden knock at the door.

It was loud and impatient, not like the knock of her neighbors in the other cottage; but the door was bolted, and the old woman rose, and shuffling to the window, looked out, and saw a shivering figure, apparently that of a youth.

'Trampers!' said the old woman, sententiously; 'tramping folk be not wanted here;' so saying, she went back to the fire without deigning to answer the door.

The youth, upon this, tried the door, and called to her to beg admittance. She heard him rap the snow from his shoes against her lintel, and again knock as if he thought she was deaf, and he should surely gain admittance if he could only make her hear.

The old woman, surprised at his audacity, went to the casement, and, with all pride of possession, opened it, and inquired his business.

'Good woman,' the stranger began, 'I only want a seat at your fire.'

'Nay,' said the old woman, giving effect to her words by her uncouth dialect, 'thoul't get no shelter here; I've nought to give to beggars—a dirty, wet *critter*,' she continued, wrathfully, slamming to the window; 'it's a wonder where he found any water, too, seeing it freezes so hard, a body can get none for the kettle, saving what's broken up with a hatchet.'

On this the beggar turned hastily away.

And at this point in his narrative, the person who told it me stopped and said, 'Do you think the old woman was very much to blame?'

'She might have acted more kindly,' I replied; 'but why do you ask?'

'Because,' said he, 'I have heard her conduct so much reflected on by some who would have thought nothing of it if it had not been for the consequences.'

'She might have turned him away less roughly,' I observed.

'That is true,' he answered; 'but, in any case, I think, though we might give them food or money, we should hardly invite beggars in to sit by the fire.'

'Certainly not,' I replied; 'and this woman could not tell that the beggar was honest.'

'No,' said he; 'but I must go on with my narrative.'

The stranger turned very hastily from her door, and waded through the deep snow towards the other cottage. The bitter wind helped to drive him towards it. It looked no less poor than the first; and, when he had tried the door, found it bolted, and knocked twice without attracting attention, his heart sank within him. His hand was so numbed with cold, that he had made scarcely any noise; he tried again.

A rush candle was burning within, and a matronly-looking woman sat before the fire. She held an infant in her arms, and had dropped asleep; but his third knock roused her, and, wrapping her apron round the child, she opened the door a very little way, and demanded what he wanted.

'Good woman,' the youth began, 'I have had the misfortune to fall in the water this bitter night, and I am so numbed that I can scarcely walk.'

The woman gave him a sudden, earnest look, and then sighed.

'Come in,' she said; 'thou art so nigh the size of my Jem, I thought at first it was him come home from sea.'

The youth stepped across the threshold, trembling with cold and wet; and no wonder, for his clothes were completely encased in wet mud, and the water dripped from them with every step he took on the sanded floor.

'Thou art in a sorry plight,' said the woman, 'and it be two miles to the nighest housen; come and kneel down afore the fire; thy teeth chatter so pitifully, I can scarce bear to hear them.'

She looked at him more attentively, and saw that he was a mere boy, not more than sixteen years of age. Her motherly heart was touched for him. 'Art hungry?' she asked, turning to the table; 'thou art wet to the skin. What hast been doing?'

'Shooting wild ducks,' said the boy.

'O,' said his hostess, 'thou art one of the keepers' boys, then, I reckon?'

He followed the direction of her eyes, and saw two portions of bread set upon the table, with a small piece of bacon upon each.

'My master be very late,' she observed, for charity did not make her use elegant language, and by her master she meant her husband; 'but thou art welcome to my bit and sup, for I was waiting for him; maybe it will put a little warmth in thee to eat and drink;' so saying, she took up a mug of beer from the hearth, and pushed it towards him, with her share of the supper.

'Thank you,' said the boy, 'but I am so wet I am making quite a pool before your fire with the drippings from my clothes.'

'Ay, thou art wet, indeed,' said the woman, and, rising again, she went to an old box, in which she began to search, and presently came to the fire with a perfectly clean checked shirt in her hand, and a tolerably good suit of clothes.

'There,' said she, showing them with no small pride, 'these be my master's Sunday clothes, and if thou wilt be *very careful of them*, I'll let thee wear them till thine be dry.' She then explained that she was going to put her 'bairn' to bed, and proceeded up a ladder into the room above, leaving the boy to array himself in these respectable and desirable garments.

When she came down her guest had dressed himself in the laborer's clothes; he had had time to warm himself, and he was eating and drinking with hungry relish. He had thrown his muddy clothes in a heap upon the floor, and, as she proceeded to lift them up, she said, 'Ah! lad, lad, I doubt thy head has been under water; thy poor mother would have been sorely frightened if she could have seen thee awhile ago.'

'Yes,' said the boy; and, in imagination, the cottage dame saw this said mother, a care-worn, hard-working creature like herself; while the youthful guest saw, in imagination, a beautiful and courtly lady; and both saw the same love, the same anxiety, the same terror at sight of a lonely boy struggling in the moonlight through breaking ice, with no one to help him, catching at the frozen reeds, and then creeping up, shivering and benumbed, to a cottage door.

But even as she stooped the woman forgot her imagination, for she had taken a waistcoat into her hands, such as had never passed between them before; a gold pencil-case dropped from the pocket, and, on the floor, among a heap of mud that covered the outer garments, lay a white shirt-sleeve, so white, indeed, and fine, that she thought it could hardly be worn but by a squire!

She glanced from the clothes to the owner. He had thrown down his cap, and his fair, curly hair, and broad forehead, convinced her that he was of gentle birth; but while she hesitated to sit down, he set a chair for her, and said, with boyish frankness, 'I say, what a lonely place this is; if you had not let me in, the water would have all frozen on me before I reached home. Catch me duck-shooting again by myself!'

'It's very cold sport that, sir,' said the woman.

The young gentleman assented most readily, and asked if he might stir the fire.

'And welcome, sir,' said the woman. She felt a curiosity to know who he was, and he partly satisfied her by remarking that he was staying at Deen Hall, a house about five miles off, adding that, in the morning, he had broken a hole in the ice very near the decoy, but it had iced over so fast, that in the dusk he had missed it and fallen in, for it would not bear him. He had made some landmarks, and taken every proper precaution, but he supposed the sport had excited him so much that, in the moonlight, he had passed them by.

He then told her of his attempt to get shelter in the other cottage.

'Sir,' said the woman, 'if you had said you were a gentleman'—

The boy laughed. 'I don't think I knew it, my good woman,' he replied, 'my senses were so benumbed; for I was some time struggling at the water's edge among the broken ice, and then I believe I was nearly an hour creeping up to your cottage door. I remember it all rather indistinctly, but as soon as I had felt the fire, and drank the warm beer, I was a different creature.'

While they still talked the husband came in, and, while he was eating his supper, they agreed that he should walk to Deen Hall, and let its inmates know of the gentleman's safety; and when he was gone they made up the fire with all the coal that remained to that poor household, and the woman crept up to bed and left her guest to lie down and rest before it.

In the gray of dawn the laborer returned, with a servant leading a horse, and bringing a fresh suit of clothes.

The young gentleman took his leave with many thanks, slipping three half-crowns into the woman's hand, probably all the money he had about him. And I must not forget to mention that he kissed the baby, for when she tells the story, the mother always adverts to that circumstance with great pride, adding, that her child being as 'clean as wax, was quite fit to be kissed by anybody!'

'Missis,' said her husband, as they stood together in the doorway, looking after their guest, 'who dost think that be?'

'I don't know,' answered the missis.

'Then I'll just tell thee, that be young Lord W——; so thou mayst be a proud woman; thou sits and talks with lords, and asks them in to supper — ha, ha!' So saying, her master shouldered his spade and went his way, leaving her clinking the three half-crowns in her hand, and considering what she should do with them. Her neighbor from the other cottage presently stepped in, and when she heard the tale and saw the money, her heart was ready to break with envy and jealousy. 'O! to think that good luck should have come to her door, and she should have been so foolish as to turn it away. Seven shillings and sixpence for a morsel of food and a night's shelter; why, it was nearly a week's wages!'

So there, as they both supposed, the matter ended, and the next week the frost was sharper than ever. Sheep were frozen in the fenny fields, and poultry on their perches, but the good woman had walked to the nearest town and bought a blanket. It was a welcome addition to their bed-covering, and it was many a long year since they had been so comfortable.

But it chanced, one day at noon, that, looking out at her casement, she spied three young gentlemen skating along the ice towards her cottage. They sprang on to the bank, took off their skates, and made for her door. The young nobleman informed her that he had had such a severe cold he could not come and see her before. 'He spoke as free and pleasantly,' she observed, in telling the story, ' as if I had been a lady, and no less! and then he brought a parcel out of his pocket, " and I've been over to B——," he says, " and bought you a book for a keepsake, and I hope you will accept it." And then they all talked as pretty as could be for a matter of ten minutes, and went away. So I waited till my master came home, and we opened the parcel, and there was a fine Bible inside, all over gold and red morocco, and my name and his name written inside ; and, bless him ! a ten-pound note doubled down over the names. I'm sure, when I thought he was a poor forlorn creature, he was kindly welcome. So my master laid out part of the money in tools, and we rented a garden, and he goes over on market days to sell what we grow ; so now, thank God, we want for nothing.'

This is how she generally concludes the little history, never failing to add that the young lord kissed her baby.

'But,' said my friend, 'I have not told you what I thought the best part of the anecdote. When this poor Christian woman was asked what had induced her to take in a perfect stranger, and trust him with the best clothing her house afforded, she answered simply, Well, I saw him shivering and shaking, so I thought " thou shalt come in here for the sake of Him that had not where to lay His head." '

Now I think we must all have read many times of such rewards following upon little acts of kindness.

Hundreds of tales are founded on such incidents, but, in real life, they are not common. Poetical justice is not the kind of justice that generally comes about in the order of God's providence. We ought not to expect such; and woful, indeed, must be the disappointment of those who do kind actions in the hope of receiving it.

The old woman in the other cottage may open her door every night of her future life to some forlorn beggar, but it is all but certain that she will never open it to a nobleman in disguise! Therefore, let neither man, woman, nor child found false hopes upon this story; for, let them entertain as many beggars as they will, they need not expect that they have gold pencil-cases in their pockets — *unless they stole them.*

These stories are, as I said, very common, and their moral is sufficiently obvious; it is, 'Do good, and you shall have your reward.' I would not quarrel with the maxim, but I should like to see it differently applied. I think it arises from a feeling which has done harm rather than good. We are, indeed, quite at liberty to use the Scriptural maxim, 'He that watereth shall be watered also himself,' but then, we should give the term 'watereth' its Scriptural sense — an extended and beautiful sense.

The act of charity is often highly valued, while the motive, which alone can make it acceptable, is overlooked and forgotten; it is not *hope* that should prompt it, but *gratitude*. Not many, even of the Lord's people, can always say in simplicity, 'I did it for the sake of Him that had not where to lay His head.'

We have strangely reversed the order of things. We sometimes act as if our feeling was, 'Let us do good and give, that God, who loveth a cheerful giver, may be good to us;' but our feeling should be, 'Christ has died, let us do good, for his sake, to his poor brethren, as an evidence that we are grateful for his inestimable gift.'

Let us do good, not to receive more good in return, but as an evidence of gratitude for what has been already bestowed. In few words, let it be 'all for love, and nothing for reward.'

www.ingramcontent.com/pod-product-compliance
Lightning Source LLC
Chambersburg PA
CBHW021836230426
43669CB00008B/986